Passport to Italian

CHARLES BERLITZ

Travel Information Supplied
by David Butwin

A SIGNET BOOK
NEW AMERICAN LIBRARY
TIMES MIRROR

SIGNET TRADEMARK REG. U.S. PAT. OFF. AND FOREIGN COUNTRIES
REGISTERED TRADEMARK—MARCA REGISTRADA
HECHO EN CHICAGO, U.S.A.

SIGNET, SIGNET CLASSICS, MENTOR, PLUME, MERIDIAN AND NAL
BOOKS are published by The New American Library, Inc.,
1633 Broadway, New York, New York 10019

First Signet Printing, April, 1974

7   8   9   10   11   12   13

PRINTED IN THE UNITED STATES OF AMERICA

 # Contents

🦅 Travel Information

When Samuel Johnson said, "A man who has not been in Italy is always conscious of inferiority," he may or may not have been exaggerating, but certainly today's visitor, like the one of three centuries ago, will find an engaging country. Things happen; people respond; inhibitions collapse. In a land of outgoing, talkative people, it's hard to distinguish the genuine from the exploitive. Yet when a tourist is taken, he has to admit it has been done with style and humor. Such is the Italian way. It makes the usual annoyances of travel seem almost enjoyable in retrospect.

Where to Stay

The traveler who finds himself in Italy after the summer mobs have left will discover that hotel rates have been uniformly slashed. Even the sleekest hotels come down to about $30 per person for a double room with two meals included. (The same rooms would cost $45 in July and August.) If your tastes are less grand, Italy has four classes of hotels below deluxe and even the first and second are generally within reason. Some second-, third-, and fourth-class hotels are classified as pensions, of which there are more than 8,000. Rates across the country are relatively stable, but standards may vary so that a third- or fourth-class hotel may have only cold running water. It's wise to inquire about such amenities beforehand. In large cities, approximate hotel prices for a single room with bath are: deluxe, $17; first class, $12; second class, $9; third class, $6; fourth class, $4.50.

Pensions (or *pensioni*), if adequately equipped, can reveal a delightful side of Italy that the first-class tourist will never see. If the mama of the house is in good form, you'll never be treated better, even at the Excelsior. She'll open the door to let you in at night, wake you up in the morning with a sweep of the curtains, and then set a breakfast tray down on the table by your bed. Of course, such attention may be too much home for some travelers. But that's the key to Italy—close touch with the people.

Although Italy claims to have more hotels than any country in the world (except the United States) and to build hotels at the fastest clip, a room in Rome in mid-July is always hard to find. So reservations for Rome, Venice, and Florence should be made far in advance.

The local tourist offices, under the heading of either EPT (Ente Provinciale Turismo) or Azienda Autonoma Turismo, will provide hotel lists and classifications, but won't book reservations. If the hunt proves tiring, you can always stop for a few hours at one of the many *alberghi diurni* or "day hotels," which, for a small fee, provide rest rooms, baths, showers, hairdressers, cleaners, and a writing den.

Recently a half-dozen holiday villages have emerged in off-track locations. Rooms go for under $10. Each village holds 600 to 800 people in several hundred cottages around a main hive of activity. Three of the busiest are the Forte village in southern Sardinia and Valtur villages in Ostuni and Isola di Capo Rizzuto in the heel and toe region. Forte has white-walled villas with wood-beam ceilings and four swimming pools, a health club, judo school, and a restaurant called Sea Lagoon Barbecue, which serves up the local marine creatures. Isola di Capo Rizzuto's village is hard by an ancient olive grove on the Ionian coast of Calabria, within hailing distance of the archeological site of Crotone and the Sila and Le Serre mountains.

How to Eat

You can always find inexpensive and plentiful food in Italy. At a rosticcerie, whose patrons usually eat standing up, an under $1 lunch might consist of either sliced meats or cheese—in other words, the contents of an antipasto. More substantial items may also be on hand, but you won't find piles of pasta drowned in tomato sauce unless a sign says *tavola calda,* or "hot table."

A trattoria, corresponding roughly to a French bistro, also provides low-cost lunches for less than $1. Food is abundant; decor is not. Lunch might include a decanter of the local *vino* (such as Chianti in Tuscany), wands of bread, and *calzone*—melted ham and cheese inside a puffy golden turnover.

An Italian picnic can be put together for less than a dollar—stop at a *salumeria* for fresh-sliced prosciutto, salami, capocollo, or mortadella; or concoct sandwiches of sliced mozarella. There is no need to settle for the supermarket variety of Italian cheese when the real thing can be found in delicatessans or cheese shops. Twenty cents will cover juices, which come in small *fiaschietti* (wicker-covered bottles). Fiaschetti also hang from stands in railroad stations and elsewhere.

What to Buy

The bargains of Florence surpass all others in Italy, and perhaps everywhere else on the Continent except Paris. Florentine products have always conjured up images of finely rendered gold and other well-wrought items. The straw markets provide greater bargains than the stores. The Porcellino market sells almost all wares cheaper than do surrounding shops. With a little nerve and charm you can usually knock down the price by a third. At Florence's open stall market around the Piazza San Lorenzo, signs may read *prezzo fisso,* "fixed price," but bargaining may still be worth a stab. Knit sweaters go for $3; leather wallets, $1-$2; purses, $2-$4. And flea-market goods, no matter how low the price, are surprisingly durable.

Savings are everywhere in Italy. Generally, the better buys are in the smaller cities. In Vicenza, for example, a dressmaker can usually whip up a request in a day or two at prices that might undercut even department store ready-to-wear items.

Northern Italy has been described as the fountainhead for contemporary furniture design, and Murano, the glass-making island near Venice, is known for its ornate chandeliers.

How to Travel

Italian State Railways, when it isn't slowed or halted by labor troubles, can roll out one of Europe's finest fleets. Its Settebello, though not part of the wide network of Trans-Europ-Express (TEE) trains, whispers between Rome and Milan in six hours, barely straining on some sections at 100 mph. By 1975 a nonstop Super Rapido run between Rome and Milan will be cut to five and a half hours, putting Florence less than ninety minutes from Rome. The Italians are also planning a breakneck run between Milan and Naples with a 160-mph peak. Bus routes usually fan out from train stations.

Italy is one of the easiest countries in Europe to explore by car without getting lost. Zippy little Fiats are everywhere on the autostradas. Any visitor who drives a vehicle registered outside of Italy can use discount gasoline coupons which cut forty percent off the usual $.92 a U.S.-gallon rate. Drivers halted by mechanical difficulty can dial a special telephone number, 116, and be towed free to the nearest repair shop, as long as it is within forty kilometers. Hitchhiking is lawful on secondary roads, but women often find Italian male drivers too accommodating hosts.

What to Do

Perhaps the greatest free sights of Italy are her celebrated piazzas. The piazza usually marks the heart of the town and has many of the city's classic sights laid out in close proximity. Around the Piazza San Marco in Venice, which Napoleon called "the most beautiful drawing room in Europe," lie the Basilica di San Marco, founded in 828 and embellished constantly until the end of the sixteenth century, and the Porta della Carta leading from the Basilica into the Doges Palace, built in florid Gothic style. Inside are masterpieces including *Paradise* by Tintoretto and three rare works by Hieronymous Bosch. But you don't have to venture indoors to appreciate San Marco and Venice. Just sitting on the steps and watching the human experience is enlightenment enough.

Museum-hopping is another way to see Italy. Since many museums have an overload of great masters of countless nationalities, tourists often opt for a preplanned tour set forth by a U.S. or Italian travel agency. The trouble with that method is that guards herd their flocks through so quickly that to blink is to miss Botticelli's *Venus* or da Vinci's *Last Supper*. A better solution is to do the tour yourself with a guidebook in hand. Some tours may leave out the best art in the city if it is too far from the mainstream or doesn't fit into the schedule. Florence tours, for instance, sometimes omit a visit to Michaelangelo's *David*, possibly the most famous work of art in the city. Pressure from the national tourist office has forced some tour guides to announce: "On this trip you will not see the statue of *David*, etc." A $1.00 museum pass can be purchased at all Alitalia and Italian Line offices, permitting the holder to visit all of Italy's most important state museums and galleries free of charge.

Closer, perhaps, to the Italian essence are street festivals. In July the Romans light up Trastevere, the old quarter across the Tiber, for the Fiesta di Noantri, the Festival of Us Others. The two most important, though not free, music festivals are the Maggio Musicale Fiorentino in Florence (May to June) and the Festival of Two Worlds at Spoleto from mid-June to mid-July, the latter dominated by the presence of Gian Carlo Menotti, the town's maestro-in-residence, and frequented by untold geniuses, including Ezra Pound in tennis sneakers. Among the most notable and spectacular of Italy's other traditional festivals, most of which are free, are the Scoppio del Carro (Firing of the Chariot) on Easter Sunday in Florence—at which a pyramid of fireworks is set off in the cathedral square by a mechanical dove driven from the Altar during High Mass; I Redentore (The Feast of the Redeemer), the third Sunday in July in Venice, a procession of gondolas and other craft commemorating the epidemic of 1575; Marostica's "Chess Game," played in the beginning of each September with living pawns and period costumes; and Piedigrotta, September 7–10, which includes parades of ornamented cars, illuminated boats and fireworks, and a Neapolitan song competition.

Another approach to Italy is to stay out of the main cities and concentrate on lesser-known places which may be rich in art and history and cost a third less. Within an hour and a half of Venice, for example, lie Padua, Vicenza, and Verona, historically and culturally prominent cities. Lake Garda, the resort, is within easy striking distance of Venice, too, but far cheaper than some of Italy's swank resorts. In fact, all you need do is draw a circle anywhere in Italy, and you'll probably encompass at least one art city, a mountain resort, and a seaside or lakeside retreat.

DAVID BUTWIN

NOTE: *Prices in dollars will vary according to whatever rate of exchange is in effect at a given time.*

🦁 Preface

Is it possible to learn to speak Italian from a phrase book? If one means basic communication—the ability to speak, understand, and generally get along—the answer is "yes," *if* you learn the right phrases. The secret of learning languages is to learn not only individual words, but the phrases in which they are apt to occur with frequency, as the Italians use them every day.

The concept of this book is to provide instant communication in Italian. The phrases are short, geared to situations of daily life, and pinpointed for easy reference, so that you can find the exact section you need at any moment.

There is even a chapter—"Words That Show You Are 'With It' "—which gives you the key words and phrases that Italian people use to add color to their conversation. In this way, instead of learning about "the umbrella of my aunt," you learn to use the right phrase at the right time, in the very way an Italian person would use it. And, so that Italian people will understand your accent, all you have to do is read the phonetic line under each Italian phrase *as if it were English*. Further practice and listening to Italian people speak will help you constantly improve your accent.

The use of this book is not limited to a trip to Italy. Italian is spoken throughout the world, and, besides the pleasure and help you will get by speaking Italian on your travels, you will find it an additional pleasure to use the idiomatic Italian you will learn in this book in Italian restaurants and with Italian-speaking people you may meet anywhere.

Young people studying Italian in a more conventional manner in school or college will find this book an invaluable aid to their studies in that it brings modern colloquial Italian alive as a means of communication.

The use of this book will more than double your enjoyment of a trip abroad and also help you save money. Besides the economic factor, why visit a foreign country if you can't break the language barrier and communicate with the new and interesting people you meet? You might as well stay home and see the palaces and monuments of the country on color TV. Who wants to be limited to one language when picking up another language can be so easy and enjoyable?

One can speak and understand current everyday Italian with comparatively few words and phrases—perhaps 1500 to 1800—which is less than the number given in the special dictionary at the end of this book. By using the same short constructions over and over, in the various situations where they normally occur, you will acquire them without conscious effort. They will become a part of your own vocabulary and of your memory bank, and that is, after all, the only secret of learning a language.

🦅 How to Acquire an Instant Accent in Italian

Every word or sentence in this book is printed first in English, then in Italian, then in an easy-to-say pronunciation system to help you to pronounce the Italian.

Just read the third line as if you were reading English and stress the syllables written in capital letters.

English: **Do you speak Italian?**

Italian: Parla Lei italiano?

Pronunciation: *PAR-la lay ee-tahl-YA-no?*

Although the following points are made clear in the third line, they will be helpful for you in pronouncing and reading Italian generally.

The vowels **a, e, i, o, u** are always pronounced *ah, eh, ee, oh, oo.* In our pronunciation system we have added an *h* to some syllables, such as *do* and *to,* to remind you to pronounce them *doh* and *toh* and not like the English words "do" and "to."

c before **e** or **i** is pronounced like English *ch;* otherwise it is pronounced *k.*

ch is pronounced like *k.*

g before **e** or **i** is pronounced as in the English "general"; otherwise as in "gave."

gh is pronounced like the *gh* in "spaghetti."

gl is pronounced like the *lli* in "million."

gn is pronounced like the *ny* in "canyon."

h is silent.

s is pronounced like an English *z* when it comes between the vowels.

sc before **e** or **i** is pronounced like English *sh;* otherwise it is pronounced *sk.*

sch is pronounced *sk.*

z is pronounced *dz* at the beginning of a word, and generally *ts* within a word.

zz is pronounced like *ts,* and occasionally like *dz.*

To give your Italian an especially authentic flavor, be sure to pronounce each double letter separately. The two *t*'s in **sette** (seven) should be sounded *SET-teh*.

With this advice, and the easy pronunciation reminder under each word, you are almost certain to be told: **Lei ha una pronuncia molto buona!** *(Lay ah OO-na pro-NOON-cha MOHL-toh BWO-na!)*, which means "You have a very good pronunciation!"

1. Greetings and Introductions

When addressing people call them **Signore, Signora,** or **Signorina,** with or *without* adding their last names. Even when you say simply **Buongiorno** it is more polite to add one of these titles to it.

Mr. (or) Sir	Mrs. (or) Madam	Miss
Signore	Signora	Signorina
seen-YO-reh	*seen-YO-ra*	*seen-yo-REE-na*

Good morning (or) Good day (or) Good afternoon, sir.
Buongiorno, signore.
bwohn-JOR-no, seen-YO-reh.

Good evening, miss.
Buona sera, signorina.
BWO-na SAIR-ra, seen-yo-REE-na.

How are you?
Come sta?
KO-meh sta?

Very well, thank you. And you?
Molto bene, grazie. E Lei?
MOHL-toh BEH-neh, GRAHTS-yeh. eh lay?

Come in.
Avanti.
ah-VAHN-tee.

Make yourself comfortable.
Si accomodi, prego.
see ahk-KO-mo-dee, PREH-go.

Your name, please?
Il Suo nome, prego?
eel SOO-wo NO-meh, PREH-go?

I am Charles Dinardo.
Io sono Carlo Dinardo.
EE-yo SO-no KAR-lo dee-NAR-doh.

May I present Mr.———
Le presento Signor———
le preh-ZEN-toh seen-YOR———

Delighted to meet you.
Piacere.
P'ya-CHEH-reh.

Goodbye.	Hi! (or) So long!	See you soon.
ArrivederLa (or)	Ciao!	A presto.
Arrivederci.	*chow!*	*ah PRESS-toh.*
ar-ree-veh-		
DAIR-la.		
ah-ree-veh-		
DAIR-chee.		

A proposito (By the way): When you say "Mr." with a man's last name, **signore** is shortened to **signor.** Mr. Dinardo—**Signor Dinardo. Signora** and **signorina** do not change.

2. Basic Expressions

Learn these by heart. You will use them every time you speak Italian to someone. If you memorize these expressions and the numbers in the next section you will find that you can ask prices, directions, and generally make your wishes known.

Yes.	No.	Perhaps.	Of course.
Sì.	No.	Forse.	Certamente.
see.	*no.*	*FOR-seh.*	*chair-ta-MEN-teh.*

Please.	Thank you.	You are welcome.
Per piacere.	Grazie.	Prego.
pair p'ya-CHEH-reh.	*GRAHTS-yeh.*	*PREH-go.*

Excuse me.	I'm sorry.	It's all right.
Mi scusi.	Mi dispiace.	Va bene.
mee SKOO-zee.	*mee dees-P'YA-cheh.*	*va BEH-neh.*

Here.	There.	This.	That.
Qui.	Là.	Questo.	Quello.
kwee.	*la.*	*KWESS-toh.*	*KWEL-lo.*

Do you speak English?	I speak Italian a little.
Parla inglese?	Parlo un po' d'italiano.
PAR-la een-GLEH-zeh?	*PAR-lo oon po dee-tahl-YA-no.*

Do you understand?	I understand.
Capisce?	Capisco.
ka-PEE-sheh?	*ka-PEE-sko.*

I don't understand.
Non capisco.
nohn ka-PEE-sko.

Very well.
Molto bene.
MOHL-toh BEH-neh.

When?
Quando?
KWAHN-doh?

How far?
Quanto è lontano?
KWAHN-toh eh lohn-TA-no?

How much time?
Quanto tempo?
KWAHN-toh TEM-po?

How?
Come?
KO-meh?

Why not?
Perchè no?
pair-KEH no?

Like this.
Così.
ko-ZEE.

Not like that.
Non così.
nohn ko-ZEE.

It is possible.
È possibile.
eh pohs-SEE-bee-leh.

It is not possible.
Non è possibile.
Nohn eh pohs-SEE-bee-leh.

Now.
Adesso.
ah-DEHS-so.

Not now.
Non adesso.
nohn ah-DEHS-so.

Later.
Più tardi.
p'yoo TAR-dee.

That's fine.
Va bene.
va BEH-neh.

It's very good.
È molto buono.
eh MOHL-toh BWO-no.

It's not good.
Non è buono.
nohn eh BWO-no.

It's very important.
È molto importante.
eh MOHL-toh eem-por-TAHN-teh.

It doesn't matter.
Non importa.
nohn eem-POR-ta.

Speak slowly, please.
Parli piano, per favore.
PAR-lee P'YA-no, pair fa-VO-reh.

Repeat, please.
Ripeta, per favore.
ree-PEH-ta, pair fa-VO-reh.

Write it.
Lo scriva.
lo SKREE-va.

Who is it?
Chi è?
kee eh?

Come in.
Avanti.
ah-VAHN-tee.

Don't come in.
Non entri.
nohn EN-tree.

Stop.
Si fermi.
see FAIR-mee.

Wait.
Aspetti.
ah-SPET-tee.

Let's go.
Andiamo.
ahn-D'YA-mo.

That's all.
È tutto.
eh TOOT-toh.

What is this?
Che cos'è questo?
keh ko-ZEH KWES-toh?

Where is the telephone?
Dov'è il telefono?
doh-VEH eel teh-LEH-fo-no?

Where is the rest-room?
Dov'è la toeletta?
doh-VEH la toh-eh-LET-ta?

... for ladies?
... per donne?
... pair DOHN-neh?

... for men?
... per signori?
... pair seen-YO-ree?

Show me.
Mi mostri.
mee MO-stree.

How much?
Quanto?
KWAHN-toh?

It's too much.
È troppo.
eh trohp-po.

Isn't it?
Non è vero?
nohn eh VEH-ro?

Who?	**I**	**you** (singular)	**you** (plural)
Chi?	io	Lei	Loro (or) voi
kee?	*EE-yo*	*lay*	*LO-ro* (or) *voy*

he	she	we	they
egli	ella	noi	essi, esse
EHL-yee	*EL-la*	*noy*	*EHS-see, EHS-say*

A proposito: You should always use **per favore**, which means "please" or, literally, "as a favor," when you ask questions or make requests. It can also function for "Bring me . . . ," "I want . . . ," or "I would like. . . ." Simply say **per favore** followed by the word for whatever you want, which you can find in the dictionary section.

Non è vero? can be used to request agreement to something or to mean "Isn't it?" "Isn't that right?" or "Don't you think so?"

🦁 3. Numbers

The numbers are important not only for asking prices (and perhaps to bargain) but also for phone numbers, addresses, and telling time. Learn the first twenty by heart and then from 20 to 100 by tens, and you can deal with **soldi** (money), **un numero di telefono** (a telephone number), **un indirizzo** (an address), and **l'ora** ("the hour," in telling time).

1	2	3	4	5
uno	due	tre	quattro	cinque
OO-no	*DOO-weh*	*treh*	*KWAHT-tro*	*CHEEN-kweh*

6	7	8	9	10
sei	sette	otto	nove	dieci
say	*SET-teh*	*OHT-toh*	*NO-veh*	*D'YEH-chee*

11	12	13
undici	dodici	tredici
OON-dee-chee	*DOH-dee-chee*	*TREH-dee-chee*

14	15	16
quattordici	quindici	sedici
kwaht-TOR-dee-chee	*KWEEN-dee-chee*	*SEH-dee-chee*

17	18	19
diciassette	diciotto	diciannove
DEE-chahs-SET-teh	*dee-CHOHT-toh*	*dee-chahn-NO-veh*

20	21	22
venti	ventuno	ventidue
VAIN-tee	*vain-TOO-no*	*vain-tee-DOO-weh*

23
ventitrè
vain-tee-TREH

24
ventiquattro
*vain-tee-
KWAHT-tro*

25
venticinque
*vain-tee-
CHEEN-kweh*

30
trenta
TRAIN-ta

40
quaranta
*kwa-
RAHN-
ta*

50
cinquanta
*cheen-
KWAHN-
ta*

60
sessanta
*sehs-SAHN-
ta*

70
settanta
*set-TAHN-
ta*

80
ottanta
*oht-TAHN-
ta*

90
novanta
*no-VAHN-
ta*

100
cento
CHEN-toh

200
duecento
*doo-weh-
CHEN-toh*

300
trecento
treh-CHEN-toh

400
quattrocento
*kwaht-tro-
CHEN-toh*

500
cinquecento
*cheen-kweh-
CHEN-toh*

600
seicento
say-CHEN-toh

700
settecento
*set-teh-
CHEN-toh*

800
ottocento
oht-toh-CHEN-toh

900
novecento
no-veh-CHEN-toh

1000
mille
MEEL-leh

2000
due mila
DOO-weh MEE-la

3000
tre mila
treh MEE-la

100,000
cento mila
CHEN-toh MEE-la

1,000,000
un milione
oon meel-YO-neh

1st	**2nd**	**3rd**
primo	secondo	terzo
PREE-mo	*seh-KOHN-doh*	*TAIRT-so*

last	**half**	**zero**
ultimo	mezzo	zero
OOL-tee-mo	*MED-zo*	*DZEH-ro*

How much?	**How many?**	**What number?**
Quanto?	Quanti?	Che numero?
KWAHN-toh?	*KWAHN-tee?*	*keh NOO-meh-ro?*

4. Arrival

Besides talking to airport officials, one of the most important things you will need to do on arrival in Italy is to find your way about. For this reason we offer you here some basic "asking your way" questions and answers and call your attention to the "Point to the Answer" sections, which the people to whom you speak can use to *point out* answers to make it easier for you to understand.

Passport, please.
Passaporto, prego.
pahs-sa-POR-toh, PREH-go.

I am on a visit.
Sono di passaggio.
SO-no dee pahs-SAHJ-jo.

For three weeks.
Per tre settimane.
Pair treh set-tee-MA-neh.

I am on a business trip.
Sono in viaggio d'affari.
SO-no in V'YAHD-jo dahf-FA-ree.

Where is the customs?
Dov'è la dogana?
doh-VEH la doh-GA-na?

Where is your baggage?
Dove sono i Suoi bagagli?
DOH-veh SO-no ee swoy ba-GAHL-yee?

My bags are over there.
Le mie valigie sono là.
leh MEE-yeh va-LEE-jeh SO-no la.

Those over there.
Quelle laggiù.
KWEL-leh lahd-JOO.

This one is mine.
Questa è mia.
KWESS-ta eh MEE-ya.

That one.
Quella.
KWEL-la.

Shall I open it?
Devo aprire?
DEH-vo ah-PREE-reh?

Open it.
Apra.
AH-pra.

There you are.
Ecco.
EHK-ko.

One moment, please.
Un momento, per piacere.
oon mo-MEHN-toh, pair p'ya-CHEH-reh.

I am looking for the key.
Sto cercando la chiave.
sto chair-KAHN-doh la K'YA-veh.

I have nothing to declare.
Non ho niente da dichia-
rare.
nohn oh N'YEN-teh da deek-ya-RA-reh.

This has been used.
Questo è usato.
KWEH-sto eh oo-ZA-toh.

These are for my personal use.
Sono oggetti personali.
SO-no oh-JET-tee pair-so-NA-lee.

These are gifts.
Sono regali.
SO-no reh-GA-lee.

Is there customs duty?
C'è dazio?
cheh DAHTS-yo?

Where is a telephone?
Dov'è un telefono?
doh-VEH oon teh-LEH-fo-no?

Where is the bus to the city?
Dov'è l'autobus per la città?
doh-VEH L'OW-toh-booss pair la cheet-TA?

Where is a restaurant?
Dov'è un ristorante?
doh-VEH oon ree-sto-RAHN-teh?

Where is the restroom?
Dov'è la toeletta?
doh-VEH la toh-eh-LET-ta?

Porter!
Facchino!
fahk-KEE-no!

Take these (bags) to a taxi.
Porti queste a un tassì.
POR-tee KWEH-steh ah oon tahs-SEE.

I'll carry this one myself.
Questa la porto io.
KWEH-sta la POR-toh EE-yo.

How much is it?
Quant'è?
kwahn-TEH?

To the Hotel Gritti.
All'Albergo Gritti.
ahl-lahl-BAIR-go GREET-tee.

To the Villa Medici.
Alla Villa Medici.
AHL-la VEEL-la MEH-dee-chee.

Excuse me, how can I go . . .
Mi scusi, che strada faccio per andare . . .
mee SKOO-zee, keh STRA-da FA-cho pair ahn-DA-reh . . .

. . . to a good restaurant?
. . . a un buon ristorante?
. . . ah oon bwohn ree-sto-RAHN-teh?

. . . to the American Consulate?
. . . al consolato americano?
. . . ahl kohn-so-LA-toh ah-meh-ree-KA-no?

. . . English?
. . . inglese?
. . . een-GLEH-zeh?

. . . Canadian?
. . . canadese?
. . . ka-na-DEH-zeh?

. . . to this address?
. . . a quest'indirizzo?
. . . ah kwehst-een-dee-REET-tso?

. . . to the movies?
. . . al cinema?
. . . ahl CHEE-neh-ma?

... to the post office?
... alla posta?
... *AHL-la PO-sta?*

... to a police station?
... alla polizia?
... *AHL-la po-leet-SEE-ya?*

... to a pharmacy?
... a una farmacia?
... *ah OO-na far-ma-CHEE-ya?*

... to a hospital?
... a un ospedale?
... *ah oon oh-speh-DA-leh?*

... to a barber?
... da un barbiere?
... *da oon barb-YEH-reh?*

... to a hairdresser?
... da un parrucchiere?
... *da oon par-rook-YEH-reh?*

Follow this street until you get to the Via Veneto.
Vada diritto fino a Via Veneto.
VA-da dee-REET toh FEE-no ah VEE-ya VEH-neh-toh.

To the right.	On the corner.	To the left.
A destra.	All'angolo.	A sinistra.
ah DEH-stra.	*ahl-LAHN-go-lo.*	*ah see-NEE-stra.*

Turn left when you get to the Piazza Vittoria.
Giri a sinistra a Piazza Vittoria.
JEE-ree ah see-NEE-stra ah P'YAHT-tsa veet-TOR-ya.

Follow Giuseppe Verdi Avenue.
Segua Viale Giuseppe Verdi.
SEH-gwa vee-YA-leh joo-SEP-peh VAIR-dee.

Is it far?	Yes.	No.	It's near.
È lontano?	Sì.	No.	È vicino.
eh lohn-TA-no?	*see.*	*no.*	*eh vee-CHEE-no.*

Thank you very much.
Grazie tante.
GRAHTS-yeh TAHN-teh.

You are very kind.
Molto gentile.
MOHL-toh jen-TEE-leh.

A proposito: When you speak to a stranger, don't forget to say **Mi scusi, signore** (or **signora** or **signorina**) before you ask a question. If you speak to a policeman call him **Guardia** (*GWAHRD-ya*).

Streets in Italy have signs on the buildings at each corner, making it easy to find out where you are.

To make sure you understand people's answers, you can show them the "Point to the Answer" sections.

🦁 5. Hotel—Laundry— Dry Cleaning

Although the staffs of the larger hotels have some training in English, you will find that the use of Italian makes for better understanding and better relations, especially with the service personnel. Besides it is fun, and you should practice Italian at every opportunity. We have included laundry and dry cleaning in this section as this is one of the things for which you have to make yourself understood in speaking to the hotel chambermaid or valet.

Can you recommend a good hotel?
Può raccomandarmi un buon albergo?
pwo rahk-ko-mahn-DAR-mee oon bwohn ahl-BAIR-go?

. . . a guest house?
. . . una pensione?
. . . OO-na pens-YO-neh?

. . . in the center of town.
. . . nel centro.
. . . nel CHEN-tro.

At a reasonable price.
A buon prezzo.
ah bwohn PREHT-tso.

I have a reservation.
Ho prenotato.
oh preh-no-TA-toh.

My name is———
Mi chiamo———
mee K'YA-mo———

Have you a room?
Ha una stanza?
ah OO-na STAHNT-sa?

I would like a room . . .
Vorrei una stanza . . .
vor-RAY OO-na STAHNT-sa . . .

. . . for one person.
. . . per una persona.
. . . pair OO-na pair-SO-na.

... for two people.
... per due persone.
... *pair DOO-weh*
   pair-SO-neh.

... with two beds.
... con due letti.
... *kohn DOO-weh*
   LET-tee.

... with a bathroom.
... con bagno.
... *kohn BAHN-yo.*

... with hot water.
... con acqua calda.
... *kohn AH-kwa KAHL-da.*

... air conditioned.
... con aria condizionata.
... *kohn AHR-ya kohn-deets-yo-NA-ta.*

... with a radio.
... con radio.
... *kohn RAHD-yo.*

... with television.
... con televisione.
... *kohn teh-leh-veez-YO-neh.*

... with a balcony.
... con terrazza.
... *kohn tehr-RAHT-tsa.*

Two communicating rooms.
Due stanze comunicanti.
DOO-weh STAHNT-seh ko-moo-nee-KAHN-tee.

How much is it?
Quanto costa?
KWAHN-toh
   KO-sta?

... per day?
... al giorno?
... *ahl JOR-no?*

... per week?
... alla settimana?
... *AHL-la settee-MA-na?*

Are the meals included?
Pranzo compreso?
PRAHNT-so kohm-PREH-zo?

Is breakfast included?
Colazione compresa?
ko-lahts-YO-neh kohm-PREH-za?

I should like to see it.
Vorrei vederla.
vor-RAY veh-DAIR-la.

Where is the bath?
Dov'è il bagno?
doh-VEH eel BAHN-yo?

. . . the shower?
. . . la doccia?
. . . la DOHT-cha?

I want another room.
Vorrei un'altra stanza.
*vor-RAY oon AHL-tra
STAHNT-sa*

. . . higher up.
. . . più in alto.
. . . p'yoo in AHL-toh.

. . . better.
. . . migliore.
*. . . meel-YO-
reh.*

. . . larger.
. . . più grande.
*. . . p'yoo
GRAHN-deh.*

. . . smaller.
. . . più piccola.
*. . . p'yoo
PEEK-ko-la.*

I'll take this room.
Prendo questa.
PREN-doh KWESS-ta.

I'll stay for five days.
Resterò per cinque giorni.
*ress-teh-RO pair CHEEN-
kweh JOR-nee.*

About one week.
Circa una settimana.
CHEER-ka OO-na set-tee-MA-na.

What time is lunch served?
A che ora è servita la colazione?
ah keh OH-ra eh sair-VEE-ta la ko-lahts-YO-neh?

What time is dinner served?
A che ora è servito il pranzo?
ah keh OH-ra eh sair-VEE-toh eel PRAHNT-so?

I would like a bottle of mineral water and ice.
Vorrei una bottiglia d'acqua minerale con ghiaccio.
*vor-RAY OO-na boht-TEEL-ya DAHK-wa
mee-neh-RA-leh kohn G'YAHT-cho.*

Send breakfast to room number 109.
Mandi la colazione alla stanza numero 109.
MAHN-dee la ko-lahts-YO-neh AHL-la STAHNT-sa
NOO-meh-ro CHEN-toh-NO-veh.

Orange juice, coffee with milk, rolls and butter.*
* For a more complete breakfast see page 38.
Succo d'arancia, caffè con latte, pane e burro.
SOOK-ko da-RAHN-cha, kahf-FEH kohn LAHT-teh,
PA-neh eh BOOR-ro.

Will you send these letters for me?
Può spedire queste lettere per me?
pwo speh-DEE-reh KWEH-steh LET-teh-reh pair meh?

Will you put stamps on them?
Può mettere i francobolli?
pwo MET-teh-reh ee frahn-ko-BOHL-lee?

The key, please.
La chiave, per favore.
la K'YA-veh, pair fa-VO-reh.

Is there any mail for me?
C'è posta per me?
cheh PO-sta pair meh?

Send my mail to this address.
Mandi le mie lettere a quest'indirizzo.
MAHN-dee leh MEE-yeh LET-teh-reh ah kwest een-dee-
REET-tso.

I want to speak to the manager.
Vorrei parlare con il direttore.
vor-RAY par-LA-reh kohn eel dee-ret-TOH-reh.

I need an interpreter.
Ho bisogno di un interprete.
oh bee-ZOHN-yo dee oon een-TAIR-preh-teh.

Are you the chambermaid?
È Lei la cameriera?
eh lay la ka-mair-YEH-ra?

I need . . .
Ho bisogno di . . .
oh bee-ZOHN-yo dee . . .

. . . a blanket.
. . . una coperta.
. . . OO-na ko-PAIR-ta.

. . . a pillow.
. . . un cuscino.
. . . oon koo-SHEE-no.

. . . a towel.
. . . un asciugamano.
. . . oon ah-shoo-ga-MA-no.

. . . soap.
. . . sapone.
. . . sa-PO-neh.

. . . toilet paper.
. . . carta igienica.
. . . KAR-ta ee-JEH-nee-ka.

This is to be dry-cleaned.
Questo è da lavare a secco.
KWESS-toh 'eh da la-VA-reh ah SEK-ko.

This is to be pressed.
Questo è da stirare.
KWESS-toh eh da stee-RA-reh.

This is to be washed.
Questo è da lavare.
KWESS-toh eh da la-VA-reh.

This is to be repaired.
Questo è da riparare.
KWESS-toh eh da ree-pa-RA-reh.

For this evening?
Per questa sera?
pair KWESS-ta SEH-ra?

. . . tomorrow?
. . . domani?
. . . doh-MA-nee?

. . . tomorrow afternoon?
. . . domani pomeriggio?
. . . doh-MA-nee po-meh-REED-jo?

. . . tomorrow evening?
. . . domani sera?
. . . doh-MA-nee SEH-ra?

When?
Quando?
KWAHN-doh?

For sure?
Di sicuro?
dee see-KOO-ro?

Be careful with this.
Faccia attenzione con questo.
FAHT-cha aht-tents-YO-neh kohn KWESS-toh.

Don't press this with a hot iron.
Non stiri questo con il ferro caldo.
nohn STEE-ree KWESS-toh kohn eel FAIR-ro KAHL-doh.

The dry cleaner.
La tintoria.
la teen-toh-REE-ya.

Are my clothes ready?
Sono pronti i miei vestiti?
so-no PROHN-tee ee M'YAY ves-TEE-tee?

Prepare my bill, please.
Mi prepari il conto, per piacere.
mee preh-PA-ree eel KOHN-toh, pair p'ya-CHEH-reh.

I'm leaving tomorrow morning.
Parto domani mattina.
PAR-to doh-MA-nee maht-TEE-na.

Can you call me at seven o'clock?
Mi può chiamare alle sette?
Mee pwo k'ya-MA-reh AHL-leh SET-teh?

It's very important.
È molto importante.
Eh MOHL-toh eem-por-TAHN-teh.

A proposito: Hotel floors are generally counted starting above the ground floor—**pianterreno**—so that the second floor is called the first, the third the second, etc.

You never have to ask for a shoeshine at a hotel. Just leave your shoes outside the door as you retire. Not a bad idea, **non è vero?** (isn't that so?)

Point to the Answer

**Per favore indichi la riposta alla mia domanda su questa
   pagina. Grazie.**
Please point to the answer to my question on this page.
   Thank you.

Oggi.	**Stasera.**	**Domani.**
Today.	This evening.	Tomorrow.

Presto.	**Tardi.**
Early.	Late.

Prima dell'una.	**Prima delle due, tre, quattro,**
Before one o'clock.	**cinque.**
	Before two, three, four, five
	o'clock.

All'una.	**Alle sei, sette, otto, nove, dieci,**
At one o'clock.	**undici, dodici.**
	At six, seven, eight, nine, ten,
	eleven, twelve o'clock.

lunedì	**martedì**	**mercoledì**	**giovedì**
Monday	Tuesday	Wednesday	Thursday

venerdì	**sabato**	**domenica**
Friday	Saturday	Sunday

6. Time: Hours—Days—Months

In the "Hotel" section you noted that when making an appointment at a certain hour you simply put **alle** in front of the number, except for "one o'clock" when you use **all'**. The following section shows you how to tell time in greater detail, including dates. You can make all sorts of arrangements with people by indicating the hour, the day, the date, and adding the phrase **Va bene?**—"Is that all right?"

What time is it?
Che ora è?
keh OH-ra eh?

It is one o'clock.
È l'una.
eh LOO-na.

It is six o'clock.
Sono le sei.
SO-no leh say.

Half past six.
Le sei e mezzo.
leh say eh MED-dzo.

A quarter past seven.
Le sette e un quarto.
leh SET-teh eh oon KWAR-toh.

A quarter to eight.
Le otto meno un quarto.
leh OHT-toh MEH-no oon KWAR-toh.

Ten minutes past ten.
Le dieci e dieci.
leh D'YEH-chee eh D'YEH-chee.

Ten minutes to three.
Le tre meno dieci.
Leh treh MEH-no D'YEH-chee.

At nine o'clock.
Alle nove.
AHL-leh NO-veh.

At exactly nine o'clock.
Alle nove in punto.
AHL-leh NO-veh een POON-toh.

in the morning
di mattina
dee maht-TEE-na

in the afternoon
di pomeriggio
dee po-meh-REED-jo

in the evening
di sera
dee SEH-ra

at night
di notte
dee NOHT-teh

today
oggi
OHD-jee

tomorrow
domani
doh-MA-nee

yesterday
ieri
YEH-ree

the day after tomorrow
dopodomani
doh-po-doh-MA-nee

the day before yesterday
ieri l'altro
YEH-ree LAHL-tro

this evening
questa sera
KWESS-ta SEH-ra

last night
ieri sera
YEH-ree SEH-ra

tomorrow evening
domani sera
doh-MA-nee SEH-ra

this week
questa settimana
KWESS-ta set-tee-MA-na

last week
la settimana scorsa
la set-tee-MA-na SKOR-sa

next week
la settimana prossima
*la set-tee-MA-na
    PROHS-see-ma*

two weeks ago
due settimane fa
*DOO-weh set-tee-MA-
    neh fa*

this month
questo mese
KWESS-toh MEH-zeh

last year
l'anno passato
LAHN-no pahs-SA-toh

next year
l'anno prossimo
LAHN-no PROHS-see-mo

five years ago
cinque anni fa
CHEEN-kweh AHN-nee fa

1970
millenovecentosettanta
MEEL-leh-no-veh-CHEN-toh-set-TAHN-ta

Monday	**Tuesday**	**Wednesday**
lunedì	martedì	mercoledì
loo-neh-DEE	*mar-teh-DEE*	*mair-ko-leh-DEE*

Thursday	**Friday**	**Saturday**	**Sunday**
giovedì	venerdì	sabato	domenica
jo-veh-DEE	*veh-nair-DEE*	*SA-ba-toh*	*doh-MEH-nee-ka*

next Monday
lunedì prossimo
loo-neh-DEE PROHS-see-mo

last Tuesday
martedì scorso
mar-teh-DEE SKOR-so

on Fridays
il venerdì
eel veh-nair-DEE

January	**February**	**March**
gennaio	febbraio	marzo
jen-NA-yo	*feb-BRA-yo*	*MART-so*

April	**May**	**June**
aprile	maggio	giugno
ah-PREE-leh	*MAHD-jo*	*JOON-yo*

July	**August**	**September**
luglio	agosto	settembre
LOOL-yo	*ah-GO-sto*	*set-TEM-breh*

October	**November**	**December**
ottobre	novembre	dicembre
oht-TOH-breh	*no-VEM-breh*	*dee-CHEM-breh*

What date?
Che data?
keh DA-ta?

March 1st
il primo marzo
eel PREE-mo MART-so

March 2nd
il due di marzo
*eel DOO-weh dee
MART-so*

3rd
il tre
eel treh

4th
il quattro
eel KWAHT-tro

the 25th of December
il venticinque di dicembre
*eel vain-tee-CHEEN-kweh
dee dee-CHEM-breh*

Merry Christmas!
Buon Natale!
bwohn nu-TA-leh!

the 1st of January
il primo gennaio
eel PREE-mo jen-NA-yo.

Happy New Year!
Buon Anno!
bwohn AHN-no!

the 15th of August
il quindici d'agosto
*eel KWEEN doo-chee
da-GO-sto*

(Have a) good vacation!
Buone vacanze!
RWO-neh va-KAHN-dzeh!

A proposito: The 15th of August is called **ferragosto,**
traditionally a day for starting one's vacation.

Italians also celebrate many feast days of particular
saints—each one called **la festa di San——** (or **Santa
——**) followed by the saint's name. These **feste** are
often marked by colorful and interesting processions.

❦ 7. Money

This section contains the vocabulary necessary for handling money. Italian bills come in denominations of 1,000, 5,000, 10,000, and 100,000 lire. Also there are coins in smaller values of lire.

Where can I change money?
Dove posso cambiare soldi?
DOH-veh POHS-so kahm-B'YA-reh SOHL-dee?

Can I change dollars here?
Posso cambiare dei dollari qui?
POHS-so kahm-B'YA-reh day DOHL-la-ree kwee?

Where is a bank?
Dove c'è una banca?
DOH-veh cheh OO-na BAHN-ka?

What time does the bank open?
A che ora si apre la banca?
ah keh OH-ra see AH-preh la BAHN-ka?

At what time does it close?
A che ora si chiude?
ah keh OH-ra see K'YOO-deh?

What's the dollar rate?
A quanto è il dollaro?
ah KWAHN-toh eh eel DOHL-la-ro?

Six hundred and twenty lire for one dollar.
Seicento venti lire al dollaro.
say-CHEN-toh VAIN-tee LEE-reh ahl DOHL-la-ro.

I want to change $50.
Voglio cambiare cinquanta dollari.
*VOHL-yo kahm-B'YA-reh cheen-KWAHN-ta
   DOHL-la-ree.*

Do you accept traveler's checks?
Accetta assegni turistici?
aht-CHET-ta ahs-SEN-yee. too-REE-stee-chee?

Of course.
Certamente.
chalr-ta-MEN-teh.

Sorry; not here.
Mi dispiace; non qui.
mee dees-P'YA-cheh; non kwee.

Will you accept my check?
Accetta un mio assegno?
aht-CHET-ta oon MEE-yo ahs-SEN-yo?

Have you identification?
Ha documenti d'identità?
ah doh-koo-MEN-tee dee-den-tee-TA?

Yes, here is my passport.
Sì, ecco il mio passaporto.
see, EK-ko eel MEE-yo pahs-sa-POR-toh.

Give me two bills of ten thousand,
Prego mi dia due biglietti da diecimila,
*preh-go mee DEE-ya DOO-weh beel-YET-tee da d'yeh-
    chee-MEE-la,*

four of five thousand and ten of a thousand.
quattro da cinquemila e dieci da mille.
*KWAHT-tro da CHEEN-kweh-MEE-la eh D'YEH-chee
    da MEE-leh.*

I need some small change.
Ho bisogno di spiccioli.
oh bee-ZOHN-yo dee SPEET-cho-lee.

8. Basic Foods

The foods and drinks mentioned in this section will enable you to be well fed, and in Italy that is very well indeed! The section that follows this will deal with special Italian dishes, representative of the cucina—"art of cooking"—that is one of the many and outstanding products of Italian culture.

breakfast
colazione
ko-lahts-YO-neh

orange juice
succo d'arancia
SOOK-ko da-RAHN-cha

grapefruit
pompelmo
pohm-PEL-mo

soft-boiled eggs
uova alla coque
WO-va AHL-la kohk

fried eggs
uova all'occhio
WO-va ahl-LOHK-k'yo

an omelet
una frittata
OO-na freet-TA-ta

scrambled eggs
uova strapazzate
WO-va stra-paht-TSA-teh

. . . with bacon
. . . con lardo
. . . kohn LAR-doh

. . . with ham
. . . con prosciutto
. . . kohn pro-SHOOT-toh

toast
pane tostato
PA-neh toh-STA-toh

coffee with hot milk
caffelatte
kahf-feh-LAHT-teh

black coffee
caffè nero
kahf-FEH NEH-ro

. . . with milk
. . . con latte
. . . kohn LAHT-teh

. . . with sugar
. . . con zucchero
. . . kohn DZOOK-keh-ro

chocolate	tea	. . . with lemon
cioccolata	tè	. . . con limone
chohk-ko-LA-ta	*teh*	. . . *kohn lee-MO-neh*

a continental breakfast (coffee, rolls, butter, marmalade)
un caffè completo
oon kahf-FEH kohm-PLEH-toh

lunch	**dinner**
colazione	pranzo
ko-lahts-YO-neh	*PRAHNT-so*

Do you know a good restaurant?
Conosce un buon ristorante?
ko-NO-sheh oon bwohn ree-sto RAHN-teh?

A table for three.	**This way, please.**
Una tavola per tre.	Da questa parte, prego.
OO-na TA-vo-la pair treh.	*da KWESS-ta PAR-teh,*
	PREH-go.

The menu, please.	**What's good?**
Il menù, prego.	Cosa c'è di buono?
eel meh-NOO, PREH-go.	*KO-za cheh dee BWO-no?*

What do you recommend?	**What is this?**
Cosa mi consiglia?	Cos'è questo?
KO-za mee kohn-SEEL-ya?	*ko-ZEH KWESS-toh?*

Good.	**I'll try it.**	**Give me this.**
Bene.	Lo proverò.	Mi dia questo.
BEH-neh.	*lo pro-veh-RO.*	*mee DEE-ya*
		KWESS-toh.

First a cocktail.	**And then some antipasto.**
Prima un aperitivo.	E poi un po d'antipasto.
PREE-ma oon ah-peh-ree-	*eh poy oon po dahn-tee-*
TEE-vo.	*PAHS-toh.*

soup	**fish**	**oysters**
minestra	pesce	ostriche
mee-NEHS-tra	*PEH-sheh*	*OH-stree-keh*

shrimps	**lobster**
scampi	aragosta
SKAHM-pee	*ah-ra-GO-sta*

roasted	**broiled**
arrosto	alla griglia
ahr-RO-sto	*AHL-la GREEL-ya*

fried	**boiled**
fritto	bollito
FREET-toh	*bohl-LEE-toh*

chicken	**duck**	**goose**
pollo	anitra	oca
POHL-lo	*AH-nee-tra*	*OH-ka*

roast pork	**pork chops**	**veal chops**
arrosto di maiale	braciole di maiale	braciole di vitello
ahr-RO-sto dee	*bra-CHO-leh dee*	*bra-CHO-leh dee*
ma-YA-leh	*ma-YA-leh*	*vee-TEL-lo*

lamb chops	**roast lamb**
braciole d'agnello	arrosto do agnello
bra-CHO-leh dahn-YEL-lo	*ahr-RO-sto dee ahn-YEL-lo*

beef	**meat balls**	**steak**
manzo	polpette	bistecca
MAHNT-so	*pohl-PET-teh*	*bee-STEK-ka*

well done	**medium**	**rare**
ben cotta	poco cotta	al sangue
ben KOHT-ta	*PO-ko KOHT-ta*	*ahl SAHN-gweh*

bread	butter	with	without
pane	burro	con	senza
PA-neh	*BOOR-ro*	*kohn*	*SENT-za*

noodles	rice	vegetables
tagliatelle	riso	legumi
tahl-ya-TEL-leh	*REE-zo*	*leh-GOO-mee*

potatoes	green beans	peas
patate	fagiolini	piselli
pa-TA-teh	*fa-jo-LEE-nee*	*pee-ZEL-lee*

carrots	spinach	tomatoes
carote	spinaci	pomodori
ka-RO-teh	*spee-NA-chee*	*po-mo-DOH-ree*

cabbage	onions	mushrooms	asparagus
cavolo	cipolle	funghi	asparagi
KA-vo-lo	*chee-POHL-leh*	*FOON-ghee*	*ahs-PA-ra-jee*

lettuce	salad	oil	vinegar
lattuga	insalata	olio	aceto
laht-TOO-ga	*een-sa-LA-ta*	*OHL-yo*	*ah-CHEH-toh*

salt	pepper	mustard	garlic
sale	pepe	senape	aglio
SA-leh	*PEH-peh*	*SEH-na-peh*	*AHL-yo*

What wine do you recommend?
Quale vino mi consiglia?
KWA-leh VEE-no mee kohn-SEEL-ya?

white wine	red wine
vino bianco	vino rosso
VEE-no B'YAHN-ko	*VEE-no ROHS-so*

beer	champagne	To your health!
birra	sciampagna	Alla sua salute!
BEER-ra	*shahm-PAHN-ya*	*AHL-la SOO-ah sa-LOO-tehl*

fruit	**grapes**	**peaches**	**apples**
frutta	uva	pesche	mele
FROOT-ta	*OO-va*	*PESS-keh*	*MEH-leh*

pears	**bananas**	**strawberries**	**oranges**
pere	banane	fragole	arance
PEH-reh	*ba-NA-neh*	*FRA-go-leh*	*ah-RAHN-cheh*

a dessert	**pastry**	**cake**
un dolce	paste	torta
oon DOHL-cheh	*PAHS-teh*	*TOHR-ta*

ice cream	**cheese**	**expresso**
gelato	formaggio	espresso
jeh-LA-toh	*for-MAHD-jo*	*ess-PRESS-so*

More, please.
Ancora, prego.
ahn-KO-ra, PREH-go.

That's enough, thank you.
Basta così, grazie.
BA-sta ko-ZEE, GRAHTS-yeh.

waiter	**waitress**
cameriere	cameriera
ka-mair-YEH-reh	*ka-mair-YEH-ra*

The check, please.
Il conto, prego.
eel KOHN-toh, PREH-go.

Is the service included?
Il servizio è compreso?
eel sair-VEETS-yo eh kohm-PREH-zo?

The bill is incorrect.
Il conto non è giusto.
eel KOHN-toh nohn eh JOOS-toh.

What do you think?   **Isn't it so?**
Che ne dice?   Non è vero?
keh neh DEE-cheh?   *nohn eh VEH-ro?*

Oh no, sir, look here.
Ah no, signore, guardi.
ah no, seen-YO-reh, GWAHR-dee.

Oh, now I understand.
Ah, adesso capisco.
ah, ah-DESS-so ka-PEES-ko.

You are right.   **It's all right.**
Ha ragione Lei.   Va bene.
ah ra-JO-neh lay.   *va BEH-neh.*

Thank you, sir.   **Come again soon!**
Grazie, signore.   Torni presto!
GRAHTS-yeh, seen-YO-reh.   *TOR-nee PRESS-toh!*

Point to the Answer

Per favore indichi la riposta alla mia domanda su questa pagina. Grazie.
Please point to the answer to my question on this page. Thank you.

Questa è la nostra specialità
This is our speciality.

È pronto.	Non è pronto.	Ci vogliono
It's ready.	It's not ready.	———minuti.
		It takes———
		minutes.

| Oggi non ne abbiamo. | Solo il sabato. |
| We don't have it today. | Only on Saturday. |

| pollo | vitello | manzo | maiale | agnello | salsice |
| chicken | veal | beef | pork | lamb | sausage |

| pesce | pasta |
| fish | spaghetti, noodles, etc. |

... con una salsa speciale
... with a special sauce

... con spaghetti
... with spaghetti

... con legumi
... with vegetables

9. Food Specialties of Italy

These expressions and names of dishes will be useful in restaurants or private homes where you may be invited. These dishes commonly appear on most Italian menus and are so much a part of Italian dining tradition that you should recognize them and know how to pronounce them as well as to enjoy them! We have written the Italian first, since that is how you will see it on the menu.

What is today's special?
Qual'è la specialità del giorno?
kwah-LEH la speh-cha-lee-TA del JOR-no?

Is it ready?
È pronto?
eh PROHN-toh?

How long will it take?
Quanto ci vorrà?
KWAHN-toh chee vor-RA?

Antipasto
ahn-tee-PA-sto
melon, ham, figs, olives, artichokes, salami

Minestrone
mee-neh-STRO-neh
vegetable soup

Timballo di riso
teem-BAHL-lo dee REE-zo
rice casserole

Cannelloni
kahn-nel-LO-nee
cheese rolled in pasta

Fettuccine al burro
feht-toot-CHEE-neh ahl BOOR-ro
noodles with butter and cheese

Risotto alla Milanese
ree-ZOHT-toh AHL-la mee-la-NEH-zeh
rice and saffron

Gnocchi alla Romana
N'YOHK-kee AHL-la ro-MA-na
dumplings baked with butter and cheese

Tagliatelle alla Bolognese
tahl-ya-TEL-leh AHL-la bo-lohn-YEH-zeh
noodles with meat sauce

Spaghetti alla carbonara
spa-GHET-tee AHL-la
  kar-bo-NA-ra
spaghetti with egg sauce

Pasticcio di lasagne
pa-STEET-cho dee
  la-SAHN-yeh
lasagna, cheese, meat

Cotolette alla Milanese
ko-toh-LET-teh AHL-la mee-la-NEH-zeh
veal, breaded and baked

Osso Buco
OHS-so BOO-ko
veal knuckles simmered with spices

Fegato alla Veneziana
FEH-ga-toh AHL-la veh-nehts-YA-na
liver with onions

Saltimbocca alla Romana
sahl-teem-BOHK-ka AHL-la ro-MA-na
veal with sage, ham, cheese, and wine

Pollo alla cacciatore
POHL-lo AHL-la kaht-cha-TOH-reh
braised chicken with black olive and anchovy sauce

Fritto Misto
FREET-toh MEES-toh
mixed seafood fried in batter

Scaloppine alla Marsala
ska-lohp-PEE-neh AHL-la mar-SA-la
veal with wine sauce

Costata alla Fiorentina
ko-STA-ta AHL-la f'yo-ren-TEE-na
ribs of beef cooked over a wood fire

Cheeses:

Bel Paese
bel pa-EH-zeh

Gorgonzola
gor-gohnd-ZO-la

Stracchino
strahk-KEE-no

Provolone
pro-vo-LO-neh

Desserts:

Torta Mille Foglie
TOR-ta MEEL-leh FOHL-yeh
pastry with cream filling

Zabaglione
dza-bahl-YO-neh
whipped eggs with brandy and sugar

Cappuccino
kahp-poot-CHEE-no
coffee with whipped cream topping

Do you like it?
Le piace?
leh PYA-cheh?

It's the best
È ottimo!
eh OHT-tee-mo!

It's excellent!
È eccellente!
eh et-chel-LEN-teh!

My congratulations to the chef (m).
Le mie congratulazioni al cuoco.
leh MEE-yeh kohn-gra-too-lahts-YO-nee ahl KWO-ko.

. . . to the cook (f).
. . . alla cuoca.
. . . AHL-la KWO-ka.

Thank you for a wonderful dinner.
Grazie per la buonissima cena.
GRAHTS-yeh pair la bwo-NEES-see-ma CHEH-na.

It's nothing. (You are welcome.)
Di niente.
dee N'YEN-teh.

I'm happy that you enjoyed it.
Sono contento che Le sia piaciuta.
so-no kohn-TEN-toh keh leh SEE-ya p'ya-CHOO-ta.

🐎 10. Transportation

Getting around by public transportation is enjoyable not only for the new and interesting things you see, but also because of the opportunities you have for practicing Italian. To make your travels easier, use short phrases when speaking to drivers or others when you ask directions. And don't forget **Prego** and **Grazie.**

Bus

Bus.
Autobus.
OW-toh-booss.

Where is the bus stop?
Dov'è la fermata dell'autobus?
*doh-VEH la fair-MA-ta
del-L'OW-toh-booss?*

Do you go to Piazza Garibaldi?
Va a Piazza Garibaldi?
va ah P'YAHT-tsa ga-ree-BAHL-dee?

No. Take number nine.
No. Prenda il numero nove.
no. PREN-da eel NOO-meh-ro NO-veh.

How much is the fare?   Where do you want to go?
Quanto costa?   Dove vuole andare?
KWAHN-toh KO-sta?   DOH-veh VWO-leh ahn-DA-reh?

To the cathedral.   Is it far?   No. It's near.
Al duomo.   È lontano?   No. È vicino.
ahl DWO-mo.   eh lohn-TA-no?   no. eh vee-CHEE-no.

Please tell me where to get off.
Per favore, mi dica dove devo scendere.
*pair fa-VO-reh, me DEE-ka DOH-veh DEH-vo
SHEN-deh-reh.*

Get off here.
Scenda qui.
SHEN-da kwee.

Point to the Answer

Per favore indichi la riposta alla mia domanda su questa pagina. Grazie.
Please point to the answer to my question on this page. Thank you.

| **Laggiù.** | **Da quella parte.** | **All'angolo.** |
| Over there. | That way. | On the corner. |

Dall'altra parte della strada.   **Diritto.**
On the other side of the street.   Straight ahead.

| **A destra.** | **A sinistra.** | **Non so.** |
| To the right. | To the left. | I don't know. |

Taxi

Taxi!	**Are you free?**
Tassì!	È libero?
tahs-SEE!	*eh LEE-beh-ro?*

Where to?	**To this address.**
Dove?	A questo indirizzo.
DOH-veh?	*ah KWESS-toh een-dee-REET-tso.*

Do you know where it is?	**I am in a hurry.**
Sa dov'è?	Ho fretta.
sa doh-VEH?	*oh FRET-ta.*

Go fast.
Vada in fretta.
VA-da een FRET-ta.

Slow down.
Vada piano.
VA-da P'YA-no.

Stop here.
Si fermi qui.
see FAIR-me kwee.

At the corner.
All'angolo.
ahl-LAHN-go-lo.

Wait for me.
Mi aspetti.
mee ah-SPET-tee.

I can't park here.
Non posso parcheggiare qui.
non POHS-so par-kehd-JA-reh kwee.

I'll be back soon.
Torno subito.
TOR-no SOO-bee-toh.

In five minutes.
Tra cinque minuti.
tra CHEEN-kweh mee-NOO-tee.

O.K.
D'accordo.
dahk-KOR-doh.

I'll wait for you.
L'aspetto.
la-SPET-toh.

How much is it per hour?
Quanto costa all'ora?
*KWAHN-toh KO-sta
ahl-LO-ra?*

. . . per kilometer?
. . . al chilometro?
. . . ahl kee-LO-meh-tro?

Call for me tomorrow.
Mi venga a prendere domani.
mee VEN-ga ah PREN-deh-reh doh-MA-nee.

In the morning.
La mattina.
la maht-TEE-na.

In the afternoon.
Il pomeriggio.
eel po-meh-REED-jo.

At three o'clock sharp.
Alle tre in punto.
*AHL-leh treh
een PUON-toh.*

At the Hotel National.
All'Albergo Nazionale.
*ahl-lahl-BAIR-go
nahts-yo-NA-leh.*

A proposito: Tip 10% or 15% of the meter. But after midnight there is a surcharge.

Point to the Answer

Per favore indichi la riposta alla mia domanda su questa pagina. Grazie.
Please point to the answer to my question on this page. Thank you.

L'aspetto aqui.
I will wait for you here.

Non posso aspettare.
I cannot wait.

Tornerò a prenderla.
I'll be back to pick you up.

Non basta.
It is not enough.

Il bagaglio è extra.
The baggage is extra.

Trains and Subway

The subway.
La metropolitana.
la meh-tro-po-lee-TA-na.

Is there a subway in this city?
C'è una metropolitana in questa città?
cheh OO-na meh-tro-po-lee-TA-na een KWESS-ta cheet-TA?

Where is the subway?
Dov'è la metropolitana?
doh-VEH la meh-tro-po-lee-TA-na?

The train.
Il treno.
eel TREH-no.

Where is the station?
Dov'è la stazione?
doh-VEH la stahts-YO-neh?

Where can I buy the tickets?
Dove posso comprare i biglietti?
DOH-veh POHS-so kohm-PRA-reh ee beel-YET-tee?

One ticket for Venice.
Un biglietto per Venezia.
oon beel-YET-toh pair veh-NEHTS-ya.

Round trip.
Andata e ritorno.
ahn-DA-ta eh ree-TOR-no.

One way only.
Andata solo.
ahn-DA-ta SO-lo.

First class.
Prima classe.
PREE-ma KLAHS-seh.

Second class.
Seconda classe.
seh-KOHN-da KLAHS-seh.

A timetable.
Un orario.
oon oh-RAR-yo.

Where is the train for Milan?
Dov'è il treno per Milano?
*doh-VEH eel TREH-no
pair mee-LA-no?*

When do we leave?
A che ora si parte?
ah keh OH-ra see PAR-teh?

Is this seat taken?
Questo posto è occupato?
*KWESS-toh PO-sto ch
ohk-koo-PA-toh?*

**With your permission,
  madam.**
Permesso, signora.
pair-MES-so, seen-YO-ra.

Of course, sir.
Certo, signore.
CHAIR-toh, seen-YO-reh.

At what time do we arrive in Florence?
A che ora arriviamo a Firenze?
ah keh OH-ra ahr-reev-YA-mo ah fee-RENT-seh?

Does the train stop in Bologna?
Si ferma il treno a Bologna?
see FAIR-ma eel TREH-no ah bo-LOHN-ya?

How long are we stopping here?
Quanto ci fermiamo qui?
KWAHN-toh chee fairm-YA-mo kwee?

Where is the dining car?
Dov'è il vagone ristorante?
doh-VEH eel va-GO-neh ree-sto-RAHN-teh?

I can't find my ticket.
Non trovo il mio biglietto.
nohn TRO-vo eel MEE-yo beel-YET-toh.

Wait!   **Here it is.**
Aspetti!   Eccolo.
ah-SPET-tee!   *EK-ko-lo.*

Prepare my berth, please.
Mi prepari la cuccetta, per favore.
mee preh-PA-ree la koot-CHET-ta, pair fa-VO-reh.

Can you help me?
Mi può aiutare?
mee pwo ah-yoo-TA-reh?

I took the wrong train.
Ho sbagliato treno.
oh zbahl-YA-toh TREH-no.

I wish to go to Naples.
Vorrei andare a Napoli.
vohr-RAY ahn-DA-reh ah NA-po-lee.

Point to the Answer

Per favore indichi la riposta alla mia domanda su questa pagina. Grazie.
Please point to the answer to my question on this page. Thank you.

Marciapiede numero————
Track number————

Da quella parte.	**Sotto.**	**Sopra.**
That way.	Downstairs.	Upstairs.

Partirà fra————minuti.
It leaves in————minutes.

Questo non è il suo treno.
This is not your train.

Non va a————.
It doesn't go to————.

Deve cambiare a————.
You must change at————.

Arrivermo alle————.
We will arrive at————o'clock.

Ship

What time does the ship sail?
A che ora parte la nave?
ah keh OH-ra PAR-tch la NA-vch?

From which pier?
Da quale banchina?
da KWA-leh bahn-KEE-na?

Where is my cabin?
Dov'è la mia cabina?
doh-VEH la MEE-ya ka-BEE-na?

Where is my luggage?
Dove sono le mie valigie?
DOH-veh SO-no leh MEE-yeh va-LEE-jeh?

Please take my luggage to my cabin.
Prego porti le mie valigie in cabina.
*PREH-go POR-tee leh MEE-yeh va-LEE-jeh
    een ka-BEE-na.*

Where is . . .	. . . the purser?	. . . the bar?
Dov'è . . .	. . . il commisario?	. . . il bar?
doh-VEH . . .	*. . . eel ko-mees-SAR-yo?*	*. . . eel bar?*

. . . the dining salon?	. . . the movie?
. . . la sala da pranzo?	. . . il cinema?
. . . la SA-la da PRAHNT-so?	*. . . eel CHEE-neh-ma?*

. . . the card room?	. . . the swimming pool?
. . . la sala da gioco?	. . . la piscina?
. . . la SA-la da JO-ko?	*. . . la pee-SHEE-na?*

first class	**tourist class**
prima classe	classe turistica
PREE-ma KLAHS-seh	*KLAHS-seh too-REES-tee-ka*

a yacht	**a motorboat**
un yacht	una barca a motore
oon yoht	*OO-na BAR-ka ah mo-TOH-reh*

a sail boat
una barca a vela
OO-na BAR-ka ah VEH-la

a ferry
un traghetto
oon tra-GHET-toh

a gondola
una gondola
OO-na GOHN-doh-la

Gondolier, sing us a song.
Gondoliere, ci canti una canzone.
*gohn-dohl-YEH-reh, chee KAHN-tee
   OO-na kahnt-SO-neh.*

🦁 11. Trips by Car

Car Rental

Where can one rent a car?
Dove si può noleggiare una macchina?
DOH-veh see pwo no-led-JA-reh OO-na MAHK-kee-na?

. . . a motorcycle?
. . . una motocicletta?
. . . OO-na mo-toh-chee-KLET-ta?

. . . a bicycle?
. . . una bicicletta?
. . . OO-na bee-chee-KLET-ta?

I want to rent a car.
Desidero noleggiare una macchina.
deh-ZEE-deh-ro no-led-JA-reh OO-na MAHK-kee-na.

How much per day?
Quanto costa al giorno?
KWAHN-toh KO-sta ahl JOR-no?

How much per kilometer?
Quanto al chilometro?
KWAHN-toh ahl kee-LO-meh-tro?

Is the gasoline included?
La benzina è compresa?
la bend-ZEE-na eh kom-PREH-za?

Is the transmission automatic?
Ha il cambio automatico?
ah eel KAHMB-yo ow-toh-MA-tee-ko?

I would like to try it out.
Vorrei provarla.
vor-RAY pro-VAR-la.

A proposito: Distances are reckoned in kilometers, approximately ⅝ of a mile.

Gas Station

Where can I buy gasoline?
Dove posso comprare della benzina?
DOH-veh POHS-so kohm-PRA-reh DEL-la bend-ZEE-na?

How much per liter?
Quanto al litro?
KWAHN-toh ahl LEE-tro?

Thirty liters, please.
Trenta litri, per piacere.
TREHN-ta LEE-tree, pair
  p'ya-CHEH-reh.

Fill it up.
Faccia il pieno.
FAHT-cha eel p'YEH-no.

Please . . .
Per favore . . .
pair fa-VO-reh . . .

Put air in the tires.
Pompi le gomme.
POHM-pee leh GOHM-meh.

Check the water.
Controlli l'acqua.
kohn-TROHL-lee
  LAHK-kwa.

. . . the battery.
. . . la batteria.
. . . la baht-teh-REE-ya.

. . . the oil.
. . . l'olio.
. . . LOHL-yo.

. . . the spark plugs.
. . . le candele.
. . . leh kahn-DEH-leh.

. . . the carburetor.
. . . il carburatore.
. . . eel kar-boo-ra-TOH-reh.

. . . the brakes.
. . . i freni.
. . . ee FREH-nee.

Change the oil.
Cambi l'olio.
KAHM-bee LOHL-yo.

Grease the motor.
Ingrassi il motore.
een-GRAHS-see eel mo-TOH-reh.

Change this tire.
Cambi questa gomma.
KAHM-bee KWESS-ta GOHM-ma.

Wash the car.
Lavi la macchina.
LA-vee la MAHK-kee-na.

A road map, please.
Una mappa stradale, prego.
OO-na MAHP-pa strah-DA-leh, PREH-go.

A proposito: Gas is sold by the liter (1.05 quarts). In other words, four liters is about one gallon.

Asking Directions

Where does this road go?
Dove va questa strada?
DOH-veh va KWESS-ta STRA-da?

Is this the way to Turin?
È questa la strada per Torino?
eh KWESS-ta la STRA-da pair toh-REE-no?

Is the road good?
È una buona strada?
eh OO-na BWO-na STRA-da?

Which is the road for Verona?
Qual'è la strada per Verona?
kwa-LEH la STRA-da pair veh-RO-na?

It's that way.
Da quella parte.
da KWEL-la PAR-teh.

Is the next town far?
È lontana la prossima città?
eh lohn-TA-na la PROHS-see-ma cheet-TA?

Do you know if there is a good restaurant there?
Sa se c'è un buon ristorante?
sa seh cheh oon bwohn ree-sto-RAHN-teh?

Is there a good hotel in Vicenza?
C'è un buon albergo a Vicenza?
cheh oon bwohn ahl-BAIR-go ah vee-CHEND-za?

Yes, there is a very good one.
Sì, ce n'è uno molto buono.
see, cheh neh OO-no MOHL-toh BWO-no.

Is it far?	**I don't know.**
È lontano?	Non lo so.
eh lohn-TA-no?	*Nohn lo so.*

About fifty kilometers.
Circa quindici chilometri.
CHEER-ka KWEEN-dee-chee kee-LO-meh-tree.

Follow this road.
Segua questa strada.
SEH-gwa KWESS-ta STRA-da.

Turn right as you leave the village.
Volti a destra all'uscita del paese.
VOHL-tee ah DESS-tra ahl-loo-SHEE-ta del pa-EH-zeh.

When you come to the bridge . . .
Quando arriva al ponte . . . .
KWAHN-doh ar-REE-va ahl POHN-teh . . .

. . . cross . . .	. . . and turn left.
. . . attraversi . . .	. . . e giri a sinistra.
. . . *aht-tra-VAIR-see* . . .	. . . *eh JEE-ree ah see-NEES-tra.*

Go straight ahead.
Vada diritto.
VA-da dee-REET-toh.

The road is not bad.
La strada non è cattiva.
la STRA-da nohn eh kaht-TEE-va.

But take the expressway.
Ma prenda l'autostrada.
ma PREN-da l'ow-toh-STRA-da.

Point to the Answer

Per favore indichi la riposta alla mia domanda su questa pagina. Grazie.
Please point to the answer to my question on this page. Thank you.

A destra.
To the right.

A sinistra.
To the left.

Diritto.
Straight ahead.

fino a . . .
until . . .

Giri a destra al prossimo semaforo.
Turn right at the next light.

Lei è in questo punto su questa carta.
You are at this point on the map.

Giri a sinistra al semaforo.
Turn left at the light.

Prosegua per questa strada.
Follow this road.

La prossima cittadina è————.
The next town is————.

Emergencies and Repairs·

Your license!	**Here it is, officer.**
La patente!	Eccola, Signor Agente!
la pa-TEN-teh!	*EK-ko-la, seen-YOR ah-JEN-teh!*

And the registration.
E i documenti della macchina.
eh ee doh-koo-MEHN-tee DEL-la MAHK-kee-na.

It wasn't my fault.	**The truck skidded.**
Non è stata colpa mia.	Il camion ha slittato.
nohn eh STA-ta KOHL-pa	*eel KAHM-yohn ah zleet-*
MEE-ya.	*TA-toh.*

This imbecile crashed into me.
Quest'imbecille mi è venuto contro.
KWEST-eem-beh-CHEEL-leh mee eh veh-NOO-toh
KOHN-tro.

A proposito: As Italians drive with considerable dash and
challenge, **imbecille, idiota, brutto,** and **cretino** (dumb
fool) are frequent and rather mild expletives. However,
control and good humor, plus a diplomatic use of Italian,
will make driving safe and enjoyable.

I need help.
Ho bisogno d'aiuto.
oh bee-ZOHN-yo da-YOO-toh.

Could you help me?
Mi può aiutare?
mee pwo ah-yoo-TA-reh?

My car has broken down.
La mia macchina non funziona.
la MEE-ya MAHK-kee-na nohn foonts-YO-na.

It's stuck.
Non va avanti.
nohn va ah-VAHN-tee.

I have a flat tire.
Ho una gomma a terra.
oh OO-na GOHM-ma ah TAIR-ra.

Can you lend me a jack?
Mi può imprestare un cricco?
mee pwo eem-press-TA-reh oon KREEK-ko?

Can you push me?
Mi può spingere?
mee pwo SPEEN-jeh-reh?

Thank you very much.	**You are very kind.**
Grazie tante.	Lei è molto gentile.
GRAHTS-yeh	*lay eh MOHL-toh*
TAHN-teh.	*jen-TEE-leh.*

I want to see the mechanic.
Voglio vedere il meccanico.
VOHL-yo veh-DEH-reh eel mek-KA-nee-ko.

He doesn't work on weekends.
Non lavora il week-end.
nohn la-VO-ra eel week-end.

What's the matter?	**The car doesn't run well.**
Che cos'è?	La macchino non va bene.
keh ko-ZEH?	*la MAHK-kee-na nohn va BEH-neh.*

There is a funny noise in the motor.
C'è un rumore strano nel motore.
cheh oon roo-MO-reh STRA-no nel mo-TOH-reh.

It's difficult to start.
È difficile metterla in moto.
eh dee-FEE-chee-leh MET-tair-la een MO-toh.

Can you fix it?	**What will it cost?**
Può aggiustarla?	Quanto costerà?
pwo ahd-joos-TAR-la?	*KWAHN-toh ko-steh-RA?*

How long will it take?
Quanto tempo ci vorrà?
KWAHN-toh TEM-po chee vor-RA?

Today isn't possible.
Oggi non è possibile.
OHD-jee nohn eh pohs-SEE-bee-leh.

Perhaps tomorrow.
Forse domani.
FOR-seh doh-MA-nee.

When will it be ready?	**In two hours.**
Quando sarà pronta?	In due ore.
KWAHN-doh sa-RA	*een DOO-weh OH-reh.*
PROHN-ta?	

Point to the Answer

**Per favore indichi la riposta alla mia domanda su questa
    pagina. Grazie.**
Please point to the answer to my question on this page.
    Thank you.

Costerà————lire.
It will cost————lire.

Sarà pronto fra————ore.
It will be ready in————hours.

Sarà pronto fra————giorni.
It will be ready in————days.

Domani.	**Dopo domani.**
Tomorrow.	The day after tomorrow.

Non abbaimo il pezzo.
We don't have the part.

Possiamo ripararla provisoriamente.
We can repair it temporarily.

International Road Signs

Danger

Caution

Sharp turn

Crossroads

Right curve

Left curve

Guarded RR
crossing

Unguarded RR
crossing

Bumps

Main road ahead

One way

Do not enter

No parking

Parking

In addition you will no doubt hear or see the following instructions:

TENERE LA DESTRA
teh-NEH-reh la DESS-tra
Keep to the right

DEVIAZIONE
dev-yahts-YO-neh
Detour

SENSO UNICO
SEN-so OO-nee-ko
One way

INCROCIO
een-KRO-cho
Crossroads

VELOCITÀ MASSIMA————CHILOMETRI
veh-lo-chee-TA MAHS-see-ma————kee-LO-meh-tree
Maximum speed————kilometers

RALLENTARE
rahl-len-TA-reh
Slow down

PARCHEGGIO VIETATO
par-KED-jo v'yeh-TA-toh
No parking

LAVORI IN CORSO
la-VO-ree een KOR-so
Road work

🦁 12. Sightseeing and Photography

We have combined these two important sections, since you will want to take pictures of what you are seeing. If you are taking pictures indoors, be sure to ask the custodian, "Is it permitted?"—E permesso?

I need a guide.
Ho bisogno di una guida.
oh bee-ZOHN-yo dee OO-na GWEE-da.

Are you a guide?
Lei è una guida?
lay eh OO-na GWEE-da?

Do you speak English?
Parla inglese?
PAR-la een-GLEH-zeh?

It doesn't matter.
Non importa.
nohn eem-POR-ta.

I speak a little Italian.
Parlo un po' d'italiano.
PAR-lo oon po dee-tahl-YA-no.

Do you have a car?
Ha una macchina?
ah OO-na MAHK-kee-na?

How much do you charge per hour?
Quanto richiede all'ora?
KWAHN-toh reek-YEH-deh ahl-LO-ra?

How much per day?
Quanto al giorno?
KWAHN-toh ahl JOR-no?

For two people?
Per due. persone?
pair DOO-weh pair-SO-neh?

A group of four?
Un. gruppo di quattro?
oon GROOP-po dee KWAHT-tro?

We would like to see the old part of the city.
Desideriamo vedere la parte vecchia della città.
deh-zee-dair-YA-mo veh-DEH-reh la PAR-teh VEHK-k'ya DEL-la cheet-TA.

Where is the Piazza Garibaldi?
Dov'è Pîazza Garibaldi?
doh-VEH p'YAHT-tsa ga-ree-BAHL-dee?

We want to go . . .
Vogliamo andare . . .
VOHL-ya-mo ahn-DA-reh . . .

. . . to the Pitti Palace.
. . . a Palazzo Pitti.
. . . ah pa-LAHT-tso PEET-tee.

. . . to the Vatican.
. . . al Vaticano.
. . . ahl va-tee-KA-no.

. . . to the Piazza Navona.
. . . a Piazza Navona.
. . . ah P'YAHT-tsa na-VO-na.

. . . to the gardens.
. . . ai giardini.
. . . I jar-DEE-nee.

. . . to the zoo.
. . . allo zoo.
. . . AHL-lo DZO-oh.

. . . to the market.
. . . al mercato.
. . . ahl mair-KA-toh.

. . . to the ruins.
. . . alle rovine.
. . . AHL-leh ro-VEE-neh.

. . . to the Cathedral.
. . . al Duomo.
. . . ahl DWO-mo.

. . . to the Roman Forum.
. . . al Foro Romano.
. . . ahl FO-ro ro-MA-no.

. . . to the Colosseum.
. . . al Colosseo.
. . . ahl ko-lohs-SEH-yo.

. . . to the Baths of Caracalla.
. . . alle Terme di Caracalla.
. . . AHL-leh TAIR-meh dee ka-ra-KAHL-la.

. . . to the Old Bridge.
. . . al Ponte Vecchio.
. . . ahl POHN-teh VEHK-k'yo.

. . . **to the Tower of Pisa.**
. . . alla Torre di Pisa.
. . . *AHL-la TOR-reh dee PEE-za.*

How beautiful!   **Very interesting!**
Che bello!   Molto interessante!
keh BEL-lo!   *MOHL-toh een-tch-ress-SAHN-tch!*

From what period is this?
Di che epoca è questo?
dee keh EH-po-ka eh KWESS-toh?

Do you know a good cabaret?
Conosce un buon locale notturno?
ko-NO-sheh oon bwohn lo-KA-leh not-TOOR-no?

Let's go.   **You are a very good guide.**
Andiamo.   Lei è un' ottima guida.
ahnd-YA-mo.   *lay eh oon OHT-tee-ma GWEE-da.*

Come again tomorrow.   **At nine o'clock sharp.**
Torni domani.   Alle nove in punto.
TOR-nee doh-MA-nee.   *AHL-leh NO-veh een*
                              POON-toh.

And, if you don't have a guide:

May one enter?   **It is open.**
Si può entrare?   È aperto.
see pwo en-TRA-reh?   *eh ah-PAIR-toh.*

It is closed.   **It opens at two o'clock.**
È chiuso.   Si apre alle due.
eh K'YOO-zo.   *see AH-preh AHL-leh DOO-weh.*

What are the visiting hours?
Qual'è l'orario delle visite?
kwu-LEH lo-RAR-yo DEL-leh VEE-zee-leh?

It is closed for repairs.
È chiuso per restauri.
eh K'YOO-zo pair rest-OW-ree.

Can one take photos?
È permesso fare fotografie?
eh pair-MESS-so FA-reh fo-toh-gra-FEE-yeh?

It is permitted.
È permesso.
eh pair-MESS-so.

It is forbidden.
È vietato.
eh v'yeh-TA-toh.

Leave your packages in the checkroom.
Lasci i pacchi al guardaroba.
LA-shee ee PAHK-kee ahl gwar-da-RO-ba.

Leave your camera.
Lasci la macchina fotografica.
LA-shee la MAHK-kee-na fo-toh-GRA-fee-ka.

What is the admission?
Quanto costa l'entrata?
KWAHN-toh KO-sta len-TRA-ta?

Two hundred lire.
Duecento lire.
Doo-weh-CHEN-toh LEE-reh.

And, for children?
E per i bambini?
eh pair ee bahm-BEE-nee?

The admission is free.
L'entrata è gratis.
len-TRA-ta eh GRA-teess.

Ticket, please.
Biglietto, prego.
beel-YET-toh, PREH-go.

Follow me.
Mi segua.
mee SEH-gwa.

This way.
Da questa parte.
da KWESS-ta PAR-teh.

This castle . . .
Questo castello . . .
KWESS-toh ka-STEL-lo . . .

This palace . . .
Questo palazzo . . .
*KWESS-toh
pa-LAHT-tso* . . .

This church . . .
Questa chiesa . . .
KWESS-ta K'YEH-za . . .

This monument . . .
Questo monumento . . .
*KWESS-toh mo-
noo-MEN-toh* . . .

This street . . .
Questa strada . . .
KWESS-ta STRA-da . . .

This square . . .
Questa piazza . . .
KWESS-ta P'YAHT-tsa . . .

What is it?
Che cos'è?
keh ko-ZEH?

It's very interesting!
È molto interessante!
*eh MOHL-toh een-teh-
ress-SAHN-teh!*

It's magnificent!
È magnifico!
eh mahn-YEE-fee-kol

It's very old, isn't it?
È molto antico, vero?
*eh MOHL-toh ahn-TEE-ko,
VEH-ro?*

This is for you.
Questo è per Lei.
KWESS-toh eh pair lay.

Some signs you may see in public places:

SIGNORI
seen-YO-ree
Men

SIGNORE
seen-YO-reh
Ladies

ENTRATA
en-TRA-ta
Entrance

USCITA
oo-SHEE-ta
Exit

APERTO
ah-PAIR-toh
Open

CHIUSO ·
K'YOO-zo
Closed

CALDO
KAHL-doh
Hot

FREDDO
FRED-doh
Cold

SPINGERE
SPEEN-geh-reh
Push

TIRARE
tee-RA-reh.
Pull

OGGETTI PERDUTI
ohd-JET-tee pair-DOO-tee
Lost and found

ORARIO DELLE VISITE
oh-RAHR-yo DEL-la VEE-zee-teh
Visiting hours

INFORMAZIONI
een-for-mahts-YO-nee
Information

GUARDAROBA
gwar-da-RO-ba
Checkroom

VIETATO FUMARE
v'yeh-TA-toh foo-MA-reh
No smoking

VIETATO ENTRARE
v'yeh-TA-toh en-TRA-reh
No admittance

A proposito: The word **vietato** in signs has the general connotation "No!" or "Don't do it!" So when you see it, don't walk on the grass, smoke, photograph, or whatever the case may be.

Photography

Where is a camera shop?
Dov'è un negozio di macchine fotografiche?
doh-VEH oon neh-GOHTS-yo dèe MAHK-kee-neh fo-toh-GRA-fee-keh?

I would like some film.
Vorrei una pellicola.
vohr-RAY OO-na pel-LEE-ko-la.

... movie film.
... un film.
... *oon film.*

... black and white.
... in bianco e nero.
... *een B'YAHN-ko eh NEH-ro.*

... in color.
... a colori.
... *ah ko-LO-ree.*

This is to be developed.
Questo è da sviluppare.
KWESS-toh eh da zvee-loop-PA-reh.

How much per print?
Quanto costa ogni fotografia?
KWAIIN-toh KO-stu OHN-yee fo-toh-gra-FEE-ya?

Two of each.
Due di ognuna.
DOO-weh dee ohn-YOO-na.

An enlargement.
Un ingrandimento.
oon een-grahn-dee-MEN-toh.

About this size.
Circa di questa misura.
CHEER-ka dee KWESS-ta mee-ZOO-ra.

When will it be ready?
Quando sarà pronto?
KWAHN-doh sa-RA PROHN-toh?

Flash bulbs.
Flash.
flahsh.

For this camera.
Per questa macchina.
pair KWESS-ta MAHK-kee-na.

It's broken.
È rotta.
eh ROHT-ta

Can you fix it?
Può aggiustarla?
pwo ad-joos-TAR-la?

May I take a photograph of you?
Le·posso fare una fotografia?
leh POHS-so FA-ray OO-na fo-toh-gra-FEE-ya?

Stand here.
Resti qui.
RESS-tee kwee.

Don't move.
Non si muova.
nohn see MWO-va.

Smile.
Sorrida.
sohr-REE-da.

That's it.
Ecco fatto.
EK-ko FAHT-toh.

Will you please take one of me?
Sia gentile, mi faccia una foto?
SEE-ya jen-TEE-leh, mee FAHT-cha OO-na FO-toh?

In front of this.
Qui davanti.
Kwee da-VAHN-tee.

You are very kind.
Lei è molto gentile.
lay eh MOHL-toh jen-TEE-leh.

May I send you a copy?
Le posso mandare una copia?
Leh POHS-so mahn-DA-reh OO-na KOHP-ya?

Your name, please?
Il Suo nome, prego?
eel SOO-wo NO-meh, PREH-go?

Your address?
Il Suo indirizzo?
eel SOO-wo een-dee-REET-tso?

A proposito: Asking to take pictures of someone often leads to more general conversation. For this reason the following three sections will be especially interesting to you.

Point to the Answer

Per favore indichi la riposta alla mia domanda su questa pagina. Grazie.
Please point to the answer to my question on this page. Thank you.

Ritorni domani.
Come back tomorrow.

Alle———ore.
At———o'clock.

Ritorni fra———giorni.
Come back in———days.

Possiamo ripararla.
We can repair it.

Non possiamo ripararla.
We cannot repair it.

Non ne abbiamo.
We haven't any.

🦁 13. Entertainment

This section will show you how to extend and accept invitations and to suggest things to do. It includes some typical conversations for theaters and night clubs and some suitable words of appreciation when you are asked for dinner.

Things to Do

May I invite you . . .
Posso invitarLa . . .
POHS-so een-vee-TAR-la . . .

. . . to lunch?
. . . a colazione?
. . . ah ko-lahts-YO-neh?

. . . to dinner?
. . . a pranzo?
. . . ah PRAHNT-so?

. . . for a drink?
. . . per un aperitivo?
. . . pair oon ah-peh-ree-TEE-vo?

. . . to go for a drive?
. . . per un giro in macchina?
. . . pair oon JEE-ro een MAHK-kee-na?

. . . to dance?
. . . a ballare?
. . . ah bahl-LA-reh?

. . . to play bridge?
. . . a giocare a bridge?
. . . ah jo-KA-reh ah breej?

. . . to the movies?
. . . al cinema?
. . . ahl CHEE-neh-ma?

. . . to the theater?
. . . a teatro?
. . . ah teh-AH-tro?

. . . to play golf?
. . . a giocare a golf?
. . . ah jo-KA-reh ah gohlf?

. . . to play tennis?
. . . a giocare a tennis?
. . . ah jo-KA-reh al
  tennis?

Thank you very much.
Grazie infinite.
GRAHTS-yeh een-fee-
  NEE-teh.

With pleasure.
Con piacere.
kohn p'ya-
  CHEH-reh.

I am sorry.
Mi dispiace.
Me dees-P'YA-
  cheh.

I cannot.
Non posso.
nohn POHS-so.

I am busy.
Sono occupato (m).
SO-no ohk-koo-PA-toh.
Sono occupata (f).
SO-no ohk-koo-PA-ta.

I am tired.
Sono stanco (m).
SO-no STAHN-ko.
Sono stanca (f).
SO-no STAHN-ka.

I am waiting for someone.
Sto aspettando qualcuno.
sto ah-spet-TAHN-doh kwahl-KOO-no.

I don't feel well.
Non mi sento bene.
nohn mee SEN-toh BEH-neh.

Maybe later.
Forse più tardi.
FOR-seh p'yoo TAR-dee.

Where are we going tomorrow?
Dove andiamo domani?
DOH-veh ahnd-YA-mo doh-MA-nee?

Let's go . . .
Andiamo . . .
ahnd-YA-mo . . .

. . . around town.
. . . in giro per la città.
. . . een JEE-ro pair la
  cheet-TA.

. . . to the opera.
. . . all'opera.
. . . ahl-LO-peh-ra.

. . . to the art museum.
. . . al museo d'arte.
. . . ahl moo-ZEH-oh
  DAR-teh.

. . . to the palace.
. . . al palazzo.
. . . *ahl pa-LAHT-tso.*

. . . to the market.
. . . al mercato.
. . . *ahl mair-KA-toh.*

. . . to the center of town.
. . . al centro.
. . . *ahl CHEN-tro.*

. . . to the park.
. . . ai giardini.
. . . *I jar-DEE-nee.*

. . . to the zoo.
. . . allo zoo.
. . . *AHL-lo DZO-oh.*

. . . to a fashion show.
. . . ad una mostra di moda.
. . . *ahd OO-na MO-stra dee MO-da.*

. . . to an art show.
. . . ad un'esposizione di quadri.
. . . *ahd oon-es-po-zeets-YO-neh dee KWAHD-ree.*

. . . for a ride in a gondola.
. . . a fare un giro in gondola.
. . . *ah FA-reh oon JEE-ro een GOHN-doh-la.*

. . . to the film festival.
. . . al festival del cinema.
. . . *ahl fes-tee-VAHL del CHEE-neh-ma.*

. . . to the movies.
. . . al cinema.
. . . *ahl CHEE-neh-ma.*

. . . to the meeting.
. . . alla riunione.
. . . *AHL-la ree-yoon-YO-neh.*

. . . to the beach.
. . . alla spiaggia.
. . . *AHL-la SP'YAHD-ja.*

. . . to the races.
. . . alle corse.
. . . *AHL-leh KOR-seh.*

. . . to the soccer game.
. . . alla partita di calcio.
. . . *AHL-la par-TEE-ta dee KAHL-cho.*

Who's ahead?
Chi sta vincendo?
kee sta veen-CHEN-doh?

Theaters and Nightclubs

Let's go to the theater.
Andiamo a teatro.
ahnd-YA-mo ah teh-AH-tro.

Two seats, please.
Due posti, per piacere.
DOO-weh PO-stee, pair p'ya-CHÈH-reh.

In the orchestra.
In platea.
een pla-TEH-ya.

In the balcony.
In galleria.
een gahl-leh-REE-ya.

Are they good seats?
Sono posti buoni?
SO-no PO-stee BWO-nee?

When does it start?
Quando comincia?
*KWAHN-doh
    ko-MEEN-cha?*

Who is playing the lead?
Chi ha la parte principale?
*kee ah la PAR-teh
    preen-chee-PA-leh?*

How beautiful she is!
Com'è bella.
ko-MEH BEL-la.

What do you think of it?
Che ne pensi?
keh neh PEN-see?

It's great.
È favoloso.
eh fa-vo-LO-zo.

I like it.
Mi piace.
mee P'YA-chee.

It's very amusing.
È molto divertente.
*eh MOHL-toh dee-vair-
    TEN-teh.*

The second act is too long.
Il secondo atto è troppo
    lungo.
*eel seh-KOHN-doh aht-toh
    eh TROHP-po LOON-go.*

(Is it) over?
Finito?
fee-NEE-toh?

Let's go to a nightclub.
Andiamo in un locale notturno.
ahnd-YA-mo een oon lo-KA-leh noht-TOOR-no.

Is there a minimum charge?
C'è un prezzo minimo?
cheh oon PRET-zo MEE-nee-mo?

A table near the dance floor.
Un tavolo vicino alla pista da ballo.
oon TA-vo-lo vee-CHEE-no AHL-la PEE-sta da BAHL-lo.

Shall we dance?
Balliamo?
bahl-L'YA-mo?

Shall we stay?
Restiamo?
rest-YA-mo?

Let's go.
Andiamo.
ahnd-YA-mo.

An Invitation to Dinner

Can you come for dinner at our house, Monday at 8?
Può venire a pranzo da noi lunedì alle otto?
*pwo veh-NEER-reh ah PRAHNT-so da noy, loo-neh-DEE
  AHL-leh OHT-toh?*

With pleasure.
Con piacere.
kohn p'ya-CHEH-reh.

If it isn't inconvenient for you.
Se non La disturba troppo.
*seh nohn la-dees-TOOR-ba
  TROHP-po.*

Sorry I'm late.
Scusi il ritardo.
*SKOO-zee eel
  ree-TAR-doh.*

The traffic was terrible!
C'era un traffico terribile!
*CHEH-ra oon TRAHF-fee-
  ko tair-REE-bee-leh!*

Very happy to see you.
Che piacere vederLa.
*keh p'ya-CHEH-reh
veh-DAIR-la.*

Make yourself at home.
Si accomodi.
see ahk-KO-mo-dee.

What a beautiful house!
Che bella casa!
keh BEL-la KA-za!

Will you have something to drink?
Desidera qualcosa da bere?
*deh-ZEE-deh-ra kwahl-KO-za
da BEH-reh?*

A cigarette?
Sigaretta?
see-ga-RET-ta?

To your health!
Alla salute!
AHL-la sa-LOO-teh!

Dinner is served.
Il pranzo è servito.
*eel PRAHNT-so eh
sair-VEE-toh.*

Will you sit here, please?
Vuole sedersi qui, per favore?
V'WO-leh seh-DAIR-see kwee, pair fa-VO-reh?

What a delicious meal!
Che pranzo squisito!
*keh PRAHNT-so skwee-
ZEE-toh!*

Do have some more!
Si serva ancora!
see SAIR-va ahn-KO-ra!

We had a wonderful time.
Ci siamo divertiti moltissimo.
chee S'YA-mo dee-vair-TEE-tee mohl-TEES-see-mo.

We must go.
Dobbiamo andare.
dohb-B'YA-mo ahn-DA-reh.

What a pity!
Che peccato!
keh pek-KA-toh!

We'll drive you back.
Vi riaccompagniamo in macchina.
vee ree-yahk-kohm-pahn-YA-mo in MAHK-kee-na.

No, please don't bother.
No, per favore non si disturbi.
no, pair fa-VO-reh nohn see dees-TOOR-bee.

Many thanks for your hospitality.
Grazie infinite per la vostra ospitalità.
*GRAHTS-yeh een-fee-NEE-teh pair la VO-stra
oh-spee-ta-lee-TA.*

Until soon.
A presto.
ah PRESS-toh.

14. Talking to People

Most phrase books are too preoccupied with attending to one's wants and generally "getting along" to pay much attention to what you should say once you have met someone. The following expressions have been tested for everyday conversational frequency and use, and, except for the rather special phrases at the end of the section, will be of immediate use for making conversation with anyone you meet.

Do you live in this city?
Abita in questa città?
AH-bee-ta een KWESS-ta cheet-TA?

Where are you from?
Da dove viene?
da DOH-veh V'YEH-neh?

I am from Milan.
Sono milanese.
SO-no mee-la-NEH-zeh.

Really?
Davvero?
dahv-VEH-ro?

What a beautiful city!
Che bella città!
keh BEL-la cheet-TA!

I've been there.
La conosco.
la ko-NO-sko.

I would like to go there.
Mi piacerebbe andarvi.
mee p'ya-cheh-REB-beh ahn-DAR-vee.

How long have you been here?
Da quanto tempo è qui?
da KWAHN-toh TEM-po eh kwee?

For three days.
Da tre giorni.
da treh JOR-nee.

Several weeks.
Da parecchie settimane.
da pa-REK-k'yeh set-tee-MA-neh.

Two months.
Da due mesi.
da DOO-weh MEH-zee.

How long will you stay here?
Quanto tempo si ferma?
KWAHN-toh TEM-po see FAIR-ma?

I will stay for one month.
Resterò un mese.
reh-steh-RO oon MEH-zeh.

Have you been here before?
È già stato qui?
eh ja STA-toh kwee?

No, never.
No, mai.
No, my.

Once.
Una volta,
OO-na VOHL-ta.

Five years ago.
Cinque anni fa.
CHEEN-kweh AHN-nee fa.

Where are you living?
Dove abita?
DOH-veh AH-bee-ta?

At what hotel?
A quale albergo?
ah KWA-leh ahl-BAIR-go?

What do you think of Rome?
Che pensa di Roma?
keh PEN-sa dee RO-ma?

I like it very much.
Mi piace molto.
mee P'YA-cheh MOHL-toh.

It's very interesting.
È molto interessante.
eh MOHL-toh een-teh-res-SAHN-teh.

It's a beautiful city.
È una bella città.
eh OO-na BEL-la cheet-TA.

The women are very beautiful.
Le donne sono molto belle.
leh DOHN-neh SO-no MOHL-toh BEL-leh.

Will you go to Florence?
Andrà a Firenze?
ahn-DRA ah fee-RENT-seh?

You must go there.
Deve andarci.
DEH-veh ahn-DAR-chee.

A proposito: When a person asks you whether you have been in certain places, you should be able to recognize the regional names, which usually resemble the English ones. Here are a few exceptions:

Venezia
veh-NEHTS-ya
Venice

Il mezzogiorno
eel med-dzo-JOR-no
the south of Italy

Il Trastevere
eel trahs-TEH-veh-reh
"The other side" of the
    Tiber, in Rome

Sicilia
see-CHEEL-ya
Sicily

Firenze
fee-RENT-seh
Florence

Do you come from the United States?
Lei viene dagli Stati Uniti?
lay V'YEH-neh DAHL-yee STA-tee oo-NEE-tee?

Yes, I am from New York.
Si, sono di Nuova York.
see, SO-no dee NWO-va
    york.

I speak a little Italian.
Parlo un po' d'italiano.
PAR-lo oon po
    dee-tahl-YA-no.

But you have a good accent.
Ma Lei ha un buon
    accento.
ma lay ah oon bwohn
    aht-CHEN-toh.

You are very kind.
Lei è molto gentile.
lay eh MOHL-toh
    jen-TEE-leh.

Have you been in the United States?
Conosce gli Stati Uniti?
ko-NO-sheh l'yee STA-tee oo-NEE-tee?

Where have you been?	**Do you like ———?**
Dov'è stato?	Le piace ———?
doh-VEH STA-toh?	*leh P'YA-cheh ———?*

What do you think of ———?
Cosa pensa di ———?
KO-za PEN-sa dee ———?

When people ask your opinion about something, you will find the following comments most helpful.

It seems to me that . . .	**In any case . . .**
Mi sembra che . . .	In ogni caso . . .
mee SEM-bra keh . . .	*een OHN-yee KA-zo . . .*

Really?	**What a shame!**
Davvero?	Che peccato!
dahv-VEH-ro?	*keh pek-KA-toh!*

I don't know.	**I have forgotten.**
Non so.	Ho dimenticato.
nohn so.	*oh dee-men-tee-KA-toh.*

I agree.	**You are right.**	**Is it possible?**
Sono d'accordo.	Ha ràgione.	È possibile?
SO-no dahk-KOR-doh.	*ah ra-JO-neh.*	*eh pohs-SEE-bee-leh?*

Very interesting.	**Magnificent.**
Molto interessante.	Magnifico.
MOHL-toh een-teh-res-SAHN-teh.	*mahn-YEE-fee-ko.*

Marvelous.	**Not bad.**
Meraviglioso.	Non è male.
meh-ra-veel-YO-zo.	*nohn eh MA-leh.*

Sometimes.
Qualche volta.
*kwahl-keh
VOHL-ta.*

Never.
Mai.
my.

Often.
Spesso.
SPEHS-so.

You must come to see us.
Deve venire a trovarci.
*DEH-veh veh-NEE-reh ah
tro-VAR-chee.*

At our house.
A casa nostra.
ah KA-za NO-stra.

With pleasure.
Con piacere.
kohn p'ya-CHEH-reh.

Are you married?
È sposato? (m)
eh spo-ZA-toh?
È sposata? (f)
eh spo-ZA-ta?

Do you have children?
Ha bambini?
ah bahm-BEE-nee?

No, I haven't.
No, non ne ho.
no, nohn neh oh.

Yes, I have.
Sì, ne ho.
see, neh oh.

How many girls?
Quante femmine?
*KWAHN-teh
FEM-mee-neh?*

How many boys?
Quanti maschi?
KWAHN-tee MAHS-kee?

How old are they?
Quanti anni hanno?
*KWAHN-tee AHN-nee
AHN-no?*

My son is seven years old.
Mio figlio ha sette anni.
*MEE-yo FEEL-yo ah
SET-teh AHN-nee.*

My daughter is ten years old.
Mia figlia ha dieci anni.
MEE-ya FEEL-ya ah D'YEH-chee AHN-nee.

What cute children!
Che bambini graziosi!
keh bahm-BEE-nee grahts-YO-zee!

This is my ...	... mother	... sister.
Questa è mia ...	... madre.	... sorella.
KWESS-ta eh	*... MA-dreh.*	*... so-REL-la.*
MEE-ya ...		

... daughter.	... wife.	... daughter-in-law.
... figlia.	... moglie.	... nuora.
... FEEL-ya.	*... MOHL-yeh.*	*... NWO-ra.*

This is my ...	... father.	... brother.
Questo è mio ...	... padre.	... fratello.
KWESS-toh eh	*... PA-dreh.*	*... fra-TEL-lo.*
MEE-yo ...		

... son.	... husband.	... son-in-law.
... figlio.	... marito.	... genero.
... FEEL-yo.	*... ma-REE-toh.*	*... JEH-neh-ro.*

Do you know ...	... that man?	... Mr. Rossi?
Conosce ...	... quell'uomo?	... il Signor Rossi?
ko-NO-sheh ...	*... kwel-LWO-mo?*	*... eel SEEN-yor ROHS-see?*

He is ..	... a writer.	... an artist.
Egli è ...	... uno scrittore.	... un artista.
EL-yee eh ...	*... OO-no skree-TOH-reh.*	*... oon ar-TEES-ta.*

... a business-
man.
... un uomo
d'affari.
... *oon WO-mo
dahf-FA-ree.*

... a lawyer.
... un avvocato.
... *oon ahv-vo-
KA-toh.*

... a doctor.
... un dottore
... *oon doht-
TOH-reh.*

... a manu-
facturer.
... un indus-
triale.
... *oon een-doo-
stree-YA-leh.*

... a military
man.
... un militare.
... *oon mee-lee-
TA-reh.*

... a painter.
... un pittore.
... *oon peet-
TOH-reh.*

... a banker.
... un ban-
chiere.
... *oon bahnk-
YEH-reh.*

... a professor.
... un pro-
fessore.
... *oon pro-fes-
SO-reh.*

... an actor.
... un attore.
... *oon aht-
TOH-reh.*

... a member of the
government.
... un membro del.
governo.
... *oon MEHM-bro del
go-VAIR-no.*

... my husband.
... mio marito.
... *MEE-yo ma-REE-toh.*

Do you know ...
Conosce ...
ko-NO-sheh ...

... that lady?
... quella sig-
nora?
... *KWEL-la
seen-YO-ra?*

... Mrs. Martin.
... la signora
Martino?
... *la seen-YO-
ra mar-TEE-
no?*

She is ...
Ella è ...
EL-la eh ...

... a writer.
... una scrittrice.
... *OO-na skreet-
TREE-cheh.*

... a singer.
... una cantante.
... *OO-na kahn-
TAHN-tch.*

... a doctor.
... una dottoressa.
... *OO-na doht-toh-RES-sa.*

... a teacher.
... una maestra.
... *OO-na ma-EHS-tra.*

... an actress.
... un'attrice.
... *oon aht-TREE-cheh.*

... my wife.
... mia moglie.
... *MEE-ya MOHL-yeh.*

He is American.
Egli è americano.
EL-yee eh ah-meh-ree-KA-no.

She is American.
Ella è americana.
EL-la eh ah-meh-ree-KA-na.

He (she) is English.
Egli (ella) è inglese.
EL-yee (EL-la) eh een-GLEH-zeh.

He is Italian.
Egli è italiano.
EL-yee eh ee-tahl-YA-no.

She is Italian.
Ella è italiana.
EL-la eh ee-tahl-YA-na.

He (she) is very intelligent.
Egli (ella) è molto intelligente.
EL-yee (EL-la) eh MOHL-toh een-tel-lee-JEN-teh.

He is very nice.
Egli è molto simpatico.
EL-yee eh MOHL-toh seem-PA-tee-ko.

She is very nice.
Ella è molto simpatica.
EL-la eh MOHL-toh seem-PA-tee-ka.

He (she) is very capable.
Egli (ella) è molto capace.
EL-yee (EL-la) eh MOHL-toh ka-PA-cheh.

This is my address.
Ecco il mio indirizzo.
EK-ko eel MEE-yo een-dee-REET-tso.

What is your address?
Qual'è il Suo indirizzo?
kwa-LEH eel SOO-wo een-dee-REET-tso?

Here is my telephone number.
Ecco il mio numero di telefono.
EK-ko eel MEE-yo NOO-meh-ro dee teh-LEH-fo-no.

What is your telephone number?
Qual'è il Suo numero di telefono?
kwa-LEH eel SOO-wo NOO-meh-ro dee teh-LEH-fo-no?

May I call you?   **When?**
La posso chiamare?   Quando?
la POHS-so k'ya-MA-reh?   *KWAHN-doh?*

Tomorrow morning.   **Early.**
Domani mattina.   Presto.
doh-MA-nee maht-TEE-na.   *PRESS-toh.*

In the afternoon.
Durante il pomeriggio.
doo-RAHN-teh eel po-meh-REED-jo.

My name is Richard.   **What is your name?**
Mi chiamo Riccardo.   Come si chiama?
mee K'YA-mo reek-KAR-   *KO-meh see K'YA-ma?*
doh.

You dance very well.
Lei balla molto bene.
lay BAHL-la MOHL-toh BEH-neh.

You sing very well.   **A voice of an angel!**
Lei canta molto bene.   Una voce d'angelo!
lay KAHN-ta MOHL-toh   *OO-na VO-cheh D'AHN-*
BEH-neh.   *jeh-lo!*

What a pretty dress!
Che bel vestito!
keh bel vess-TEE-toh!

I have a surprise for you.
Ho una sorpresa per Lei.
oh OO-na sor-PREH-za pair lay.

Do you like it?
Le piace?
leh P'YA-cheh?

Can we see each other again?
Possiamo rivederci?
pohs-S'YA-mo ree-veh-DAIR-chée?

When?
Quando?
KWAHN-doh?

Where?
Dove?
DOH-veh?

What's the matter?
Cosa è successo?
KO-za eh soot-CHEHS-so?

Are you angry?
È arrabbiata? (to a woman)
eh ahr-rahb-B'YA-ta?
È arrabbiato? (to a man)
eh ahr-rahb-B'YA-toh?

Why?
Perchè?
pair-KEH?

Where are you going?
Dove va?
DOH-veh va?

Let's go together.
Andiamo insieme.
ahnd-YA-mo een-S'YEH-meh.

I like you very much.
Ho molta simpatia per Lei.
oh MOHL-ta seem-pa-TEE-ya pair lay.

You are very beautiful.
Lei è molto bella.
lay eh MOHL-toh BEL-la.

You are very nice.
Lei è molto gentile. (to a man)
lay eh MOHL-toh jen-TEE-leh.
Lei è molto carina. (to a woman)
lay eh MOHL-toh ka-REE-na.

I like you very much.
Ho molto simpatia per te.
oh MOHL-toh seem-pa-TEE-ya pair teh.

Are you serious?
Sul serio?
sool SEHR-yo?

And how do you feel?   **I (feel) the same.**
E tu, cosa ne pensi?   Anch'io.
eh too, KO-za neh PEN-see? ahn-KEE-yo.

I love you.
Ti amo.
tee AH-mo.

Will you give me your photo?
Mi dai una tua foto?
mee dye OO-na TOO-wa FO-toh?

Will you write to me?   **Don't forget!**
Mi scriverai?   Non dimenticare!
mee skree-veh-RYE?   nohn dee-men-tee-KA-reh!

A proposito: In the last sentences we have used the familiar form for "you," both in the verb and in the pronoun, since the tone of the conversation implies a certain degree of familiarity.

🦁 15. Words That Show You Are "With It"

There are certain words that Italian-speaking people use constantly but that do not always have an exact equivalent in English. To use them at the right time will make Italian people feel that you have not only à diploma in good manners but also an excellent foundation in Italian culture patterns—in other words, that you are "with it." The Italian words and phrases are given first to make it easier for you to recognize them as they occur in everyday conversation.

We have divided these terms into two groups. The first is composed of selected polite expressions:

Bravo! (m) or Brava! (f)
BRA-vo!, BRA-va!
Good for you!

Congratulazioni!
kohn-gra-too-lahts-YO-nee!
Congratulations!

Complimenti!
kohm-plee-MEN-tee!
My compliments!

Auguri!
ow-GOO-ree!
Best wishes!

Alla salute!
AHL-la sa-LOO-teh!
To your health!

Buon viaggio!
bwohn V'YAHD-jo!
Have a good trip!

Si diverta!
see dee-VAIR-ta!
Have a good time!

Saluti a ———!
sa-LOO-tee ah ———!
Regards to ———!

Si accomodi!
see ahk-KO-mo-dee!
Make yourself comfortable!

To someone eating or about to eat:

Buon appetito!
bwohn ah-peh-TEE-toh!
Good appetite!

When someone sneezes:

Salute!
sa-LOO-teh!
Health!

To wish someone good luck:

Buona fortuna! *(or)*		**In bocca al lupo!**
BWO-na for-TOO-na!		*een BOHK-ka ahl LOO-po!*
Good luck!		Into the mouth of the wolf!

To which one may reply:

Crepi il lupo!
KREH-pee eel LOO-po!
May the wolf burst!

Since the following phrases permeate conversation, it will interest you to know what they mean, as well as to learn to employ them as useful conversational stopgaps. The translations are quite free, as these expressions are very idiomatic.

Ma . . . !	**Così-così.**
ma . . . !	*ko-ZEE ko-ZEE.*
But . . . ! *or* Now, wait a minute!	So-so.

Poi . . .	**Non è vero?**
poy . . .	*nohn eh VEH-ro?*
And then . . .	Isn't it? *or* Don't you think so?

Più o meno.
p'yoo oh MEH-no.
More or less.

Andiamo!
ahnd-YA-mo!
Let's go! *or* Come on!

Vediamo un po'!
vehd-YA-mo oon po!
Let's see!

Allora . . .
uh-LO-ra . . .
Then . . .

Dai!
dye!
Come on! Keep going!

Va bene!
va BEH-neh!
It's O.K.!

Dunque . . .
DOON-kweh . . .
Well, now . . .

Ebbene . . .
eb-BEH-neh . . .
Well, now . . .

Cosa c'è di nuovo?
KO-za cheh dee N'WO-vo?
What's new?

Niente affatto.
N'YEN-teh ahf-FAHT-toh.
Nothing at all.

Ma no!
ma no!
You don't say! *or* Not at all!

Che figura!
keh fee-GOO-ra!
Bad show!

C'è qualcosa che non va?
cheh kwahl-KO-za keh nohn va?
Is something wrong?

Va via!
va VEE-ya!
Go away!

Ma insomma . . .
ma een-SOHM-ma . . .
But after all . . .

Non fa niente!
nohn fa N'YEN-teh!
It doesn't matter!

Non vale la pena.
nohn VA-leh la PEH-na.
It's not worth while.

Favoloso!
fa-vo-LO-zo!
Great!

Fenomenale!
fe-no-meh-NA-leh!
Great!

Santo cielo!
SAHN-toh CHEH-lo!
Good heavens!

Perbacco!
pair-BAHK-ko!
Good heavens! (literally
   "By Bacchus!")

Mamma mia!
MAHM-ma MEE-ya!
Good heavens! (literally
   "My mother!")

Si figuri!
see fee-GOO-ree!
Just imagine!

16. Shopping

Shops in Italy still tend to be specialized, although there exist chains of general stores and even the supermarket—supermercato.

Names of Shops

Where can I find . . .
Dove posso trovare . . .
DOH-veh POHS-so tro-VA-reh . . .

. . . the department stores?
. . . i grandi magazzini?
. . . ee GRAHN-dee ma-gahd-DZEE-nee?

. . . a dress shop?
. . . un negozio di abbigliamento?
. . . oon neh-GOHTS-yo dee ahb-beel-ya-MEN-toh?

. . . a hat shop?
. . . un negozio di cappelli?
. . . oon neh-GOHTS-yo dee kahp-PEL-lee?

. . . a shoe store?
. . . un negozio di calzature?
. . . oon neh-GOHTS-yo dee kahl-tsa-TOO-reh?

. . . a perfume shop?
. . . una profumeria?
. . . OO-na pro-foo-meh-REE-ya?

. . . a jewelry shop?
. . . una gioielleria?
. . . OO-na joy-yel-leh-REE-ya?

. . . a drugstore?
. . . una farmacia?
. . . OO-na far-ma-CHEE-ya?

. . . a bookshop?
. . . una libreria?
. . . OO-na lee-breh-REE-ya?

. . . a toy shop?
. . . un negozio di giocattoli?
. . . oon neh-GOHTS-yo dee jo-KAHT-toh-lee?

. . . a flower shop?
. . . un fioraio?
. . . oon f'yo-RA-yo?

. . . an antique shop?
. . . un negozio di antichità?
. . . *oon neh-GOHTS-yo dee ahn-tee-kee-TA?*

. . . a grocery store?   **. . . a market?**
. . . un negozio di alimen-   . . . un mercato?
tari?   . . . *oon mair-KA-toh?*
. . . *oon neh-GOHTS-yo*
dee ah-lee-men-TA-ree?

. . . a camera shop?
. . . un negozio di articoli fotografici?
. . . *oon neh-GOHTS-yo dee ar-TEE-ko-lee fo-toh-GRA-fee-chee?*

. . . a tobacco shop?   **. . . a barber shop?**
. . . una tabaccheria?   . . . un barbiere?
. . . *OO-na ta-bahk-keh-*   . . . *oon barb-YEH-reh?*
REE-ya?

. . . a beauty shop?
. . . un parrucchiere?
. . . *oon par-rook-K'YEH-reh?*

A proposito: Some additional shop signs you will see in Italy include **Gelateria** (ice cream parlor), **Salumeria** (a shop specializing in delicious sausages), and **Trattoria** (a small informal restaurant). In certain small shops **da** (at the house of) precedes a proper name. **Da Mario** means "at Mario's house" or "at Mario's shop."

General Shopping Vocabulary

May I help you?   **What do you wish?**
Posso aiutarLa?   Che cosa desidera?
POHS-so ah-yoo-TAR-la?   *keh KO-za deh-ZEE-deh-ra?*

I would like to buy . . .
Desidero comprare . . .
*deh-ZEE-deh-ro kohm-
PRA-reh . . .*

. . . a gift for my husband.
. . . un regalo per mio
marito.
*. . . oon reh-GA-lo pair
MEE-yo ma-REE-toh.*

. . . a gift for my wife.
. . . un regalo per mia moglie.
. . . oon reh-GA-lo pair MEE-ya MOHL-yeh.

. . . something for a man.
. . . una cosa per uomo.
*. . . OO-na KO-za pair
WO-mo.*

. . . something for a lady.
. . . una cosa per donna.
*. . . OO-nu KO-za pair
DOHN-na.*

Nothing for the moment.
Niente per ora.
N'YEN-teh pair OH-ra.

I'm just looking around.
Voglio solo guardare.
*VOHL-yo SO-lo gwahr-DA-
reh.*

I'll be back later.
Torno più tardi.
*TOR-no p'yoo
TAR-dee.*

I like this.
Mi piace questo.
*mee P'YA-cheh
KWESS-toh.*

. . . that.
. . . quello.
. . . KWEL-lo

How much is it?
Quanto costa?
KWAHN-toh KO-sta?

Show me another.
Me ne mostri un altro.
*meh neh MO-stree oon
AHL-tro.*

Something less expensive.
Qualche cosa di meno
costoso.
*KWAHL-keh KO-za dee
MEH-no ko-STO-zo.*

Do you like this?
Le piace questo?
*leh P'YA-cheh KWESS-
toh?*

May I try it on?
Posso provarlo?
POIIS-so pro-VAR-lo?

That suits you marvelously.
Le sta benissimo.
leh sta beh-NEES-see-mo.

Good. I'll take it.
Va bene. Lo prendo.
va BEH-neh. lo PREN-doh.

Can you alter it?
Può fare delle riparazioni?
*pwo FA-reh DEL-leh
ree-pah-rahts-YO-nee?*

Is it handmade?
È fatto a mano?
eh FAHT-toh ah MA-no?

Is it hand-embroidered?
È ricamato a mano?
*eh ree-ka-MA-toh ah
MA-no?*

Will you wrap it?
Può incartarlo?
pwo een-kar-TAR-lo?

Can one pay by check?
Si può pagare con un
assegno?
*see pwo pa-GA-reh kohn
oon ahs-SEHN-yo?*

Can you send it to this address?
Può mandarlo a quest'indirizzo?
pwo mahn-DAR-lo ah kwest-een-dee-REET-tso?

A receipt, please.
Una ricevuta, per favore.
*OO-na ree-cheh-VOO-ta,
pair fa-VO-reh.*

The change, please.
Il resto, per favore.
*eel REHS-toh, pair
fa-VO-reh.*

**Come see us
again!**
Ritorni presto!
*ree-TOHR-nee
PRESS-toh!*

Sale
Svendita
ZVEN-dee-ta

Bargain sale!
Prezzi bassi!
*PRET-tsee
BAHS-see*

Point to the Answer

**Per favore indichi la riposta alla mia domanda su questa
pagina. Grazie.**
Please point to the answer to my question on this page.
Thank you.

Non ne abbiamo.
We haven't any.

È tutto quello che abbiamo.
It's all we have.

Non ne abbiamo più grandi.
We haven't any larger.

Non ne abbiamo più piccoli.
We haven't any smaller.

Non mandiamo a casa.
We don't deliver.

Possiamo spedirlo in America.
We can send it to America.

Qual'è il Suo indirizzo?
What is your address?

Non accettiamo un assegno personale.
We don't accept personal checks.

Accettiamo assegni turistici.
We accept traveler's checks.

Clothes

a suit	**a coat**	**a scarf**
un vestito	un cappotto	una sciarpa
oon vess-TEE-toh	*oon kahp-POHT-toh*	*OO-na SHAR-pa*
a hat	**gloves**	**shoes**
un cappello	guanti	scarpe
oon kahp-PEL-lo	*GWAHN-tee*	*SKAR-peh*

boots
stivali
stee-VA-lee

an umbrella
un ombrello
oon ohm-BREL-lo

a raincoat
un impermeabile
oon eem-pair-meh-AH-bee-leh

pajamas
un pigiama
oon pee-JA-ma

a bathrobe
una vestaglia
OO-na vess-TAHL-ya

slippers
pantofole
pahn-TOH-fo-leh

a swimsuit
un costume da bagno
oon ko-STOO-meh da BAHN-yo

sandals
sandali
SAHN-da-lee

a handkerchief
un fazzoletto
oon-faht-tso-LET-toh

a blouse
una blusa
OO-na BLOO-za

a skirt
una gonna
OO-na GOHN-na

a handbag
una borsa
OO-na BOHR-sa

stockings
calze
KAHLD-zeh

a slip
una sottoveste
OO-na soht-toh-VESS-teh

a brassiere
un regiseno
oon red-jee-SEH-no

panties
mutandine
moo-tahn-DEE-neh

a nightgown
una camicia da notte
OO-na ka-MEE-cha da NOHT-teh

an evening dress
un vestito da sera
oon vess-TEE-toh da SEH-ra

an evening coat
un cappotto da sera
oon kahp-POHT-toh da SEH-ra

a shirt
una camicia
OO-na ka-MEE-cha

pants
i pantaloni
ee pahn-ta-LO-nee

a jacket
una giacca
OO-na JAHK-ka

a tie
una cravatta
OO-na kra-VAHT-ta

socks
i calzetti
ee kahld-ZET-tee

an undershirt
una canotticra
OO-na ka-noht-T'YEH-ra

undershorts
mutande
moo-TAHN-deh

Sizes—Colors—Materials

What size?
Di che misura?
*dee keh mee-
SOO-ra?*

small
piccolo, -a*
PEEK-ko-lo, -la

medium
medio, -a
MEHD-yo, -ya

* If the article referred to is masculine (see dictionary) the
adjective ends in **o**, if feminine, in **a**.

large
grande
GRAHN-deh

extra large
extra grande
EX-tra GRAHN-deh

larger
più grande
*p'yoo GRAHN-
deh*

smaller
più piccolo, -a
*p'yoo PEEK-
ko-lo, -la*

wider
più largo, -a
*p'yoo LAR-
go, -gu*

narrower
più stretto, -a
*p'yoo STRET-
toh, -ta*

longer
più lungo, -a
*p'yoo LOON-
go, -ga*

shorter
più corto, -a
*p'yoo KOHR-
to, -ta*

What color?
Di che colore?
*dee keh
ko-LO-rch?*

red
rosso, -a
ROHS-so, -sa

blue
blu
bloo

yellow
giallo, -a
JAHL-lo, -la

orange
arancione
ah-rahn-CHO-neh

green
verde
VAIR-deh

violet
violetto, -a
v'yo-LET-toh, -ta

brown
marrone
mar-RO-neh

gray
grigio, -a
GREE-jo, ja

black
nero, -a
NEH-ro, -ra

white
bianco, -a
B'YAHN-ko, -ka

beige
beige
beige

darker
più scuro, -a
p'yoo SKOO-ro, -ra

lighter
più chiaro, -a
p'yoo K'YA-ro, -ra

Is it silk?
È di seta?
eh dee SEH-ta?

. . . linen?
. . . lino?
. . . LEE-no?

. . . velvet?
. . . velluto?
. . . vel-LOO-toh?

. . . wool?
. . . lana?
. . . LA-na?

. . . cotton?
. . . cotone?
. . . ko-TOH-neh?

. . . lace?
. . . merletti?
. . . mair-LET-tee?

. . . leather?
. . . cuoio?
. . . KWO-yo?

. . . suede?
. . . camoscio?
. . . ka-MO-sho?

. . . kid?
. . . pelle?
. . . PEL-leh?

. . . plastic?
. . . plastica?
. . . PLAHS-tee-ka?

. . . fur?
. . . pelliccia?
. . . pel-LEET-cha?

What kind of fur?
Che pelliccia è?
keh pel-LEET-cha eh?

fox
volpe
VOHL-peh

beaver
castoro
ka-STO-ro

seal	mink	leopard
foca	visone	leopardo
FO-ka	*vee-SO-neh*	*leh-oh-PAR-doh*

Newsstand

I would like . . .
Vorrei . . .
vor-RAY. . .

. . . a guide book.
. . . una guida.
. . . *OO-na GWEE-da.*

. . . a map of the city.
. . . una mappa della città.
. . . *OO-na MAHP-pa DEL-la cheet-TA.*

. . . sunglasses.
. . . occhiali da sole.
. . . *ohk-K'YA-lee da SO-leh.*

. . . some postcards.
. . . delle cartoline.
. . . *DEL-leh kar-toh-LEE-neh.*

. . . this newspaper.
. . . questo giornale.
. . . *KWESS-toh jor-NA-leh.*

. . . that magazine.
. . . questa rivista.
. . . *KWESS-ta re-VEE-sta.*

. . . a newspaper in English.
. . . un giornale in inglese.
. . . *oon jor-NA-leh een een-GLEH-zeh.*

Tobacco Shop

Have you American cigarettes?
Ha delle sigarette americane?
ah DEL-leh see-ga-RET-teh ah-meh-ree-KA-neh?

cigars
sigari
SEE-ga-ree

a pipe
una pipa
OO-na PEE-pa

tobacco
tabacco
ta-BAHK-ko

matches
fiammiferi
f'yahm-MEE-feh-ree

a lighter
un accendisigaro
oon aht-chen-dee-SEE-ga-ro

a refill
un ricambio
oon ree-KAHMB-yo

Drugstore

I would like . . .
Vorrei . . .
vohr-RAY . . .

a toothbrush
uno spazzolino da denti
*OO-no spaht-tso-LEE-no
   da DEN-tee.*

toothpaste
dentifricio
den-tee-FREE-cho

a razor
un rasoio
oon ra-ZOY-yo

razor blades
lamette
la-MET-teh

shaving cream
sapone da barba
sa-PO-neh da BAR-ba

cologne
colonia
ko-LOHN-ya

a hairbrush
una spazzola
OO-na SPAHT-tso-la

a comb
un pettine
oon pet-TEE-neh

aspirin
aspirina
ah-spee-REE-na

some iodine
dell'iodio
del-L'YOHD-yo

scissors
forbici
FOR-bee-chee

a nail file
una lima da unghie
*OO-na LEE-ma da
    OON-ghee-yeh*

some antiseptic
dell'antisettico
del-lahn-tee-SET-tee-ko

Band Aids
cerotti
cheh-ROHT-tee

coughdrops
pastiglie per la tosse
pahs-TEEL-yeh pair la TOHS-seh

Cosmetics

I would like . . .
Vorrei . . .
vohr-RAY . . .

powder
cipria
CHEEP-r'ya

lipstick
rossetto .
rohs-SET-toh

eye shadow
ombretto
ohm-BRET-toh

nail polish
smalto
ZMAHL-toh

perfume
profumo
pro-FOO-mo

an eyebrow pencil
una matita per gli occhi
OO-na ma-TEE-ta pair l'yee OHK-kee

cotton
cotone
ko-TOH-neh

bobby pins
forcine
for-CHEE-neh

hair-spray
lacca
LAHK-ka

That smells good, doesn't it?
Che buon odore, vero?
keh bwohn oh-DOH-reh, VEH-ro?

Hairdresser

a shampoo
uno shampù
OO-no shahm-POO

and set
e messa in piega
eh MEHS-sa een P'YEH-ga

a manicure
una manicura
OO-na ma-nee-KOO-ra

a tint
una tintura
OO-na teen-TOO-ra

lighter
più chiara
p'yoo K'YA-ra

darker
più scura
p'yoo SKOO-ra

It's too hot!
È troppo caldo!
eh TROHP-po KAHL-doh!

Barber

shave
barba
BAR-ba

and haircut
e capelli
eh ka-PEL-lee

a massage
un massaggio
oon mahs-SAHD-jo

Use scissors.
Usi le forbici.
OO-zee leh FOR-bee-chee.

shorter
più corto
p'yoo KOR-toh

not too short
non troppo corto
nohn TROHP-po KOR-toh

the top
il davanti
eel da-VAHN-tee

the back
il dietro
eel D'YEH-tro

the sides
i lati
ee LA-tee

That's fine.
Così va bene.
ko-ZEE va BEH-neh.

Where do I pay?
Dove devo pagare?
DOH-veh DEH-vo pa-GA-reh?

Food Market

I would like ...
Vorrei ...
vor-RAY ...

... a dozen
... una dozzina
... *OO-na dohd-ZEE-na*

... of these.
... di questi.
... *de KWESS-tee.*

... of those.
... di quelli.
... *dee KWEL-lee.*

I want five of them.
Ne voglio cinque.
*neh VOHL-yo
    CHEEN-kweh.*

Is this fresh?
È fresco questo?
eh FREH-sko KWESS-toh?

Three cans of this.
Tre barattoli di questo.
*treh ba-RAIIT-toh-lee dee
    KWESS-toh.*

How much per kilo?
Quanto al chilo?
KWAIIN-toh ahl KEE-lo?

What kind of wine do you
    have?
Che vino ha?
keh VEE-no ah?

All kinds.
Tutti.
TOOT-tee.

What is this?
Cos'è questo?
ko-ZEH KWESS-toh?

Please put it all in a bag.
Per favore metta tutto in
    un sacchetto.
*pair fa-VO-reh MET-ta
    TOOT-toh een oon
    sahk-KET-toh.*

A proposito: Weight is measured by the kilo—chilo—
(kilogram—chilogramma) rather than by the pound. One
kilo is equivalent to 2.2 pounds.

Jewelry

I would like to see . . .	. . . a watch.	. . . a ring.
Vorrei vedere . . .	. . . un orologio.	. . . un anello.
vor-RAY veh-DEH-reh . . .	*oon oh-ro-LO-jo.*	*oon ah-NEL-lo.*

. . . a necklace.	. . . a bracelet.
. . . una collana.	. . . un braccialetto.
. . . OO-na kohl-LA-na.	*. . . oon braht-cha-LET-toh.*

. . . some earrings.
. . . degli orecchini.
. . . DEL-yee oh-rehk-KEE-nee.

Is this gold?	. . . platinum?	. . . silver?
È d'oro?	. . . di platino?	. . . d'argento?
eh DOH-ro?	*. . . dee PLA-tee-no?*	*. . . dar-JEN-toh?*

Is it silver-plated?	Is it gold-plated?
È argentato?	È dorato?
eh ar-jen-TA-toh?	*eh doh-RA-toh?*

a diamond	a pearl	a ruby
un brillante	una perla	un rubino
oon breel-LAHN-teh	*OO-na PAIR-la*	*oon roo-BEE-no*

a sapphire	an emerald
uno zaffiro	uno smeraldo
OO-no DZAHF-fee-ro	*OO-no zmeh-RAHL-doh*

Is this real?	. . . or an imitation?
È autentico?	. . . o un' imitazione?
eh ow-TEN-tee-ko?	*. . . oh oon ee-mee-tahts-YO-neh?*

Antiques

What period is this?
Di che epoca è questo?
dee keh EH-po-ka eh
  KWESS-toh?

It's beautiful.
È molto bello.
eh MOHL-toh BEL-lo.

But very expensive.
Ma molto caro.
ma MOHL-toh KA-ro.

How much is ...
Quanto costa ...
KWAHN-toh KO-sta ...

... this book?
... questo libro?
... KWESS-toh LEE-bro?

... this picture?
... questo quadro?
... KWESS-toh
  KWA-dro?

... this map?
... questa mappa?
... KWESS-ta MAHP-pa?

... this frame?
... questa cornice?
... KWESS-ta
  kor-NEE-cheh?

... this piece of furniture?
... questo mobile?
... KWESS-toh MO-bee-leh?

Is it an antique?
È antico?
eh ahn-TEE-ko?

Can you ship it?
Può spedirlo?
pwo speh-DEER-lo?

To this address?
A questo indirizzo?
ah KWESS-toh een-dee-REET-tso?

🦗 17. Telephone

Talking on the phone is an excellent test of your ability to communicate in Italian because you can't see the person you are talking to nor use gestures to help get across your meaning. When asking for someone, simply say his name and add **prego**. If you say the number instead of dialing, say the numbers in pairs: 3536 would be 35–36, or **trentacinque–trentasei**.

Where is the telephone?
Dov'è il telefono?
do-VEH eel teh-LEH-fo-no?

The telephone operator.
La telefonista.
la teh-leh-fo-NEES-ta.

Hello!
Pronto!
PROHN-toh!

Who is speaking?
Chi parla?
kee PAR-la?

Information.
Informazioni.
een-for-mahts-YO-nee.

Please, the telephone number of ——.
Per favore, il numero di telefono di ——.
pair fa-VO-reh, eel NOO-meh-ro dee teh-LEH-fo-no dee ——.

Long distance.
Interurbana.
een-tair-oor-BA-na.

Get me number —— in Rome.
Mi dia il numero —— a Roma.
mee DEE-ya eel NOO-meh-ro ——ah RO-ma.

I would like to call New York, in the United States.
Vorrei chiamare Nuova York, negli Stati Uniti.
vohr-RAY k'ya-MA-reh NWO-va york, NEL-yee STA-tee
oo-NEE-tee.

I am calling number ———.
Sto chiamando il numero ———.
sto k'ya-MAHN-doh eel NOO-meh-ro ———.

Extension ———.
Interno ———.
een-TAIR-no ———.

How long must I wait?
Quanto devo aspettare?
KWAHN-toh DEH-vo ahs-pet-TA-reh?

How much is it per minute?
Quanto costa al minuto?
KWAHN-toh KO-sta ahl mee-NOO-toh?

My number is ———.
Il mio numero è ———.
eel ME-yo NOO-meh-ro eh ———.

Mr. (Mrs.) Rossi, please.
Il signor (la signora) Rossi, per piacere.
eel seen-YOR (la seen-YO-ra) ROHS-see, pair
p'ya-CHEH-reh.

What?
Come?
KO-meh?

He (she) isn't here.
Non c'è.
nohn cheh.

Hold on.
Attenda.
aht-TEN-da.

When is he (she) coming back?
Quando sarà di ritorno?
KWAHN-do sa-RA dee ree-TOR-no?

Very well, I'll call back.
Grazie, richiamerò.
GRAHTS-yeh, reek-ya-meh-RO.

Can I leave a message?
Posso lasciare un messaggio?
POHS-so la-SHA-reh oon mess-SAHD-jo?

Ask him (her) to call me.
Gli (le) dica di chiamarmi.
l'yee (leh) DEE-ka dee k'ya-MAR-mee.

I'll give you my number.
Le do il mio numero.
leh doh eel MEE-yo NOO-meh-ro.

This is Mr. Verga speaking.
Parla il signor Verga.
PAR-la eel seen-YOR VAIR-ga.

That is spelled V–E–R–G–A.
Si scrive V–E–R–G–A.
see SKREE-veh vee–eh–EHR-reh–jee–ah.

A	B	C	D
ah	*bee*	*chee*	*dee*

E	F	G	H
eh	*EF-feh*	*jee*	*AHK-ka*

I	J	K	L
ee	*ee-LOON-ga*	*KAHP-pa*	*el-LEH*

M	N	O	P
EM-meh	*EN-neh*	*oh*	*pee*

Q	R	S	T
koo	*EHR-reh*	*ES-seh*	*tee*

U	V	W	X
oo	*vee*	*DOHP-p'ya-vee*	*iks*

Y	Z
ee-GREH-ka	*DZAY-ta*

A proposito: As American and English names are often strange to Italian ears, you will find the spelled-out alphabet very useful for spelling your name when you leave a message.

Where is a public telephone?
Dov'è il telefono pubblico?
doh-VEH eel teh-LEH-fo-no POOB-blee-ko?

... the telephone book?
... l'elenco telefonico?
... leh-LEN-ko teh-leh-FO-nee-ko?

What do I put in?
Cosa metto dentro?
KO-za MET-toh DEN-tro?

How much do I owe you?
Quanto Le devo?
KWAHN-toh leh DEH-vo?

In Italy tokens are used in public telephones.

A token, please.
Un gettone, per favore.
oon jet-TOH-neh, pair fa-VO-reh.

Another token.
Un altro gettone.
oon AHL-tro jet-TOH-neh.

If there is no public telephone available:

May I use your phone?
Potrei usare il Suo telefono?
po-TRAY oo-ZA-reh eel SOO-wo teh-LEH-fo-no?

Certainly.
Certamente.
chair-ta-MEN-teh.

🦁 18. Post Office and Telegrams

One of the first things one does when abroad is to write postcards—**cartoline postale**—to friends and relatives. Here is how to mail them. You might also impress your friends by adding a few words in Italian, which you will find at the end of this section.

Where is the post office?
Dov'è la posta?
doh-VEH la POHS-ta?

Ten stamps of ten lire.
Dieci francobolli da dieci lire.
D'YEH-chee frahn-ko-BOHL-lee da D'YEH-chee LEE-reh.

How much is needed?
Quanti ce ne vogliono?
KWAHN-tee cheh neh VOHL-yo-ne?

... for air mail?
... per via aerea?
... pulr VEE-ya ah-EH-reh-ya?

For a letter to the United States.
Per una lettera per gli Stati Uniti.
pair OO-na LEH-teh-ra pair l'yee STA-tee oon-NEE-tee.

... to England.
... per l'Inghilterra.
... pair leen-geel-TEHR-ra.

... to Canada.
... per il Canada.
... pair eel ka-na-DA.

... to Spain.
... per la Spagna.
... pair la SPAHN-ya.

... to Germany.
... per la Germania.
... pair la jair-MAHN-ya.

... to Yugoslavia.
... per la Jugoslavia.
... *pair la joo-*
  go-SLAHV-ya.

... to France.
... per la Francia.
... *pair la FRAHN-cha.*

... to Austria.
... per l'Austria.
... *pair L'OW-stree-ya.*

... to Greece.
... per la Grecia.
... *pair la GREH-cha.*

For names of other countries, see dictionary.

a registered letter
una lettera raccomandata
OO-na LET-teh-ra
  rahk-ko-mahn-DA-ta

an insured parcel
un pacco assicurato
oon PAHK-ko ahs-see-
  koo-RA-toh

Where can I send a telegram?
Dove posso mandare un telegramma?
DOH-veh POHS-so mahn-DA-reh oon
  tel-leh-GRAHM-ma?

How much is it per word?
Quanto costa alla parola?
KWAHN-toh KO-sta AHL-la pa-RO-la?

I need writing paper ...
Ho bisogno di carta da
  lettere ...
oh bee-ZOHN-yo dee
  KAR-ta da LET-teh-reh.

... envelopes.
... buste.
... *BOO-steh.*

Can you lend me ...
Mi può imprestare ...
mee pwo eem-pres-TA-reh ...

... a pen?
... una penna?
... *OO-na PEN-na?*

... a pencil?
... una matita?
... *OO-na ma-TEE-ta?*

. . . some stamps?
. . . dei francobolli?
. . . *day frahn-ko-BOHL-lee?*

Dear John,
Caro Giovanni,
KA-ro jo-VAHN-nee,

Dear Jane,
Cara Giovanna,
KA-ra jo-VAHN-na,

Best regards from Naples.
Saluti da Napoli.
sa-LOO-tee da NA-po-lee.

I miss you.
Sento la Sua mancanza.
SEN-toh la SOO-wa
mahn-KAHN-tsa.

Best wishes to everyone.
Saluti a tutti.
sa-LOO-tee ah TOOT-tee.

Fondly,
Caramente,
ka-ra-MEN-teh,

ᨠᨂ 19. The Weather

winter
l'inverno
leen-VAIR-no

spring
la primavera
la pree-ma-VEH-ra

summer
l'estate
leh-STA-teh

autumn
l'autunno
low-TOON-no

How is the weather?
Com'è il tempo?
ko-MEH eel TEM-po?

The weather is fine.
È bel tempo.
eh bel TEM-po.

It's cold.
Fa freddo.
fa FRED-doh.

It's raining.
Piove.
P'YO-veh.

It's very hot.
Fa molto caldo.
fa MOHL-toh KAHL-doh.

Let's go swimming.
Andiamo a nuotare.
ahn-D'YA-mo ah nwo-TA-reh.

Where is the pool?
Dov'è la piscina?
doh-VEH la pee-SHEE-na?

I need an umbrella.
Ho bisogno di un ombrello.
oh bee-ZOHN-yo dee oon ohm-BREL-lo.

. . . a raincoat.
. . . un impermeabile.
. . . oon eem-pair-mee-AH-bee-leh.

. . . boots.
. . . stivali.
. . . stee-VA-lee.

What a fog!
Che nebbia!
keh NEHB-b'ya!

One can't see anything.
Non si vede niente.
nohn see VEH-deh N'YEN-teh.

It's snowing.	Do you like to ski?	. . . to skate?
Nevica.	Le piace sciare?	. . . pattinare?
neh-VEE-ka.	*leh P'YA-cheh SHAH-reh?*	*. . . paht-tee-NA-reh?*

I want to rent a pair of skis.	. . . skates.
Desidero noleggiare un paio di sci.	. . . pattini.
deh-ZEE-deh-ro no-led-JA-reh oon PA-yo dee shee.	*. . . PAHT-tee-nee.*

A proposito: Temperature is expressed in centigrade, not Fahrenheit. Zero is freezing in centigrade, and 100° is boiling. To change centigrade to Fahrenheit, multiply by ⅑ and add 32°; to change Fahrenheit to centigrade, subtract 32° and multiply by ⅝.

Doctor

I am ill.
Mi sento male.
mee SEN-toh MA-leh.

My wife ...
Mia moglie ...
MEE-ya MOHL-yeh ...

My husband ...
Mio marito ...
MEF-yo ma-
 REE-toh ...

My daughter ...
Mia figlia ...
MEE-ya
 FEEL-ya ...

My son ...
Mio figlio ...
MEE-yo
 FEEL-yo ...

My friend ...
Il mio amico (m) ...
eel MEE-yo
 ah-MEE-ko ...
La mia amica (f) ...
la MEE-ya ah-MEE-ka ...

... is ill.
... si sente male.
... see SEN-teh MA-leh.

We need a doctor.
C'è bisogno di un dottore.
cheh bee-ZOHN-yo dee
 oon doht-TOH-reh.

When can he come?
Quando può venire?
KWAHN-doh pwo
 veh-NEE-reh?

Well, what's wrong with you?
Allora, cosa succede?
ahl-LO-ra, KO-za soot-CHEH-deh?

I don't feel well.
Non mi sento bene.
nohn mee SEN-toh BEH-neh.

Where does it hurt?
Dove Le fa male?
DOH-veh leh fa MA-leh?

Here.
Qui.
kwee.

I have a pain . . .
Ho mal . . .
oh mahl . . .

He (she) has a pain . . .
Lui (lei) ha mal . . .
lwee (lay) ah mahl . . .

. . . in the head.
. . . di testa.
. . . dee TEH-sta.

. . . in the throat.
. . . di gola.
. . . dee GO-la.

. . . in the ear.
. . . d'orecchio.
. . . doh-REHK-kee-oh.

. . . in the
stomach.
. . . di stomaco.
*. . . dee
STO-ma-ko.*

. . . in the back.
. . . di schiena.
*. . . dee
SK'YEH-na.*

I hurt my leg.
Mi sono fatto male alla gamba.
mee SO-no FAHT-toh MA-leh AHL-la GAHM-ba.

. . . my foot.
. . . al piede.
*. . . ahl
P'YEH-deh.*

. . . my arm.
. . . al braccio.
*. . . ahl
BRAHT-cho.*

. . . my hand.
. . . alla mano.
*. . . AHL-la
MA-no.*

I am dizzy.
Mi gira la testa.
mee JEE-ra la TEH-sta.

I can't sleep.
Non posso dormire.
*nohn POHS-so
dor-MEE-reh.*

I have a fever.
Ho la febbre.
oh la FEB-breh.

I have diarrhea.
Ho la diarrea.
oh la dee-yar-REH-ya.

Since when?
Da quando?
da KWAHN-doh?

Since yesterday.
Da ieri.
da YEH-ree.

Since two days ago.
Da due giorni.
da DOO-weh JOR-nee.

What have you eaten?
Che cosa ha mangiato?
keh KO-za ah mahn-JA-toh?

Undress.
Si spogli.
see SPOHL-yee.

Lie down.
Si distenda.
see dee-STEN-da.

Sit up.
Si sieda.
see S'YEH-da.

Breathe deeply.
Respiri a fondo.
reh-SPEE-ree ah
  FOHN-doh.

Open your mouth.
Apra la bocca.
AH-pra la BOHK-ka.

Show me your tongue.
Mi mostri la lingua.
mee MO-stree la LEEN-gwa.

Cough.
Tossisca.
tohs-SEES-ka.

Say "thirty-three."
Dica "trentatrè."
DEE-ka TRAIN-ta-treh.

Get dressed.
Si vesta.
see VEH-sta.

You must stay in bed.
Deve stare a letto.
DEH-veh STA-reh ah LET-toh.

You must go to the hospital.
Deve andare all'ospedale.
DEH-veh ahn-DA-reh ahl-lo-speh-DA-leh.

Take this prescription.
Prenda questa ricetta.
PREN-da KWESS-ta ree-CHET-ta.

Take these pills.
Prenda queste pastiglie.
PREN-da KWESS-teh pa-STEEL-yeh.

Is it serious?
È grave?
eh GRA-veh?

It's not serious.
Non è grave.
nohn eh GRA-veh.

Don't worry.
Non si preoccupi.
nohn see preh-OHK-koo-pee.

You have . . .
Lei ha . . .
lay ah . . .

. . . indigestion.
. . . un indigestione.
. . . oon een-dee-jest-YO-neh.

. . . an infection.
. . . un'infezione.
. . . oon-een-fehts-YO-neh.

... a cold.
... un
raffreddore.
... *oon rahf-
fred-DOR-reh.*

... liver trouble.
... mal di
fegato. ·
... *mahl tlee
FEH-ga-toh.*

... appendicitis.
... l'appendicite.
... *la-pen-dee-
CHEE-teh.*

... a heart attack.
... un attacco cardiaco.
... *oon aht-TAHK-ko
kard-EE-ah-ko.*

Be careful.
Stia attento.
STEE-ya aht-TEN-toh.

Don't eat too much.
Non mangi troppo.
nohn MAHN-gee TROHP-po.

Don't drink any alcoholic drinks.
Non prenda bevande alcooliche.
nohn PREN-da beh-VAHN-deh ahl-ko-OH-lee-keh.

Except wine, of course.
Eccetto il vino,
naturalmente.
*et-CHET-toh eel VEE-no,
na-too-rahl-MEN-teh.*

How do you feel today?
Come si sente oggi?
*KO-meh see SEN-teh
OHD-jee?*

The same.
Lo stesso.
lo STES-so.

Better.
Meglio.
MEHL-yo.

Much better.
Molto meglio.
*MOHL-toh
MEHL-yo.*

A proposito: The centigrade scale (see p. 130) is also used to measure body temperature. The normal body temperature is 36.7 degrees. So if you have anything higher than that, you have a fever—Lei ha febbre.

Dentist

In the unlikely event that the dentist should hurt you, tell him Si fermi!—"Stop!"—or Aspetti un momento!— "Wait a moment!" This will give you time to regain your courage.

Can you recommend a dentist?
Può raccomandarmi un dentista?
pwo rahk-ko-mahn-DAR-mee oon den-TEES-ta?

I have a toothache.
Ho mal di denti.
oh mahl dee DEN-tee.

It hurts here.
Mi fa male qui.
mee fa MA-leh kwee.

You need a filling.
Ha bisogno di un'otturatura.
ah bee-ZOHN-yo dee oon-oht-too-ra-TOO-ra.

Just fix it temporarily.
Me lo aggiusti provvisoriamente.
meh lo ahd-JOO-stee prohv-vee-zohr-ya-MEN-teh.

How long will it take?
Quanto tempo ci vuole?
KWAHN-toh TEM-po chee VWO-leh?

A few minutes.
Pochi minuti.
PO-kee mee-NOO-tee.

There is an infection.
C'è un'infezione.
cheh oon-een-fehts-YO-neh.

I must extract this tooth.
Dobbiamo togliere questo dente.
dohb-B'YA-mo TOHL-yeh-reh KWESS-toh DEN-teh.

An anesthetic, please.
Per favore, un anestetico.
pair fa-VO-reh, oon ah-nes-TEH-tee-ko.

Does it hurt?	**A little.**	**Not at all.**
Fa male?	Un poco.	Per niente.
fa MA-leh?	*oon PO-ko.*	*pair N'YEN-teh.*

Is it finished?
È finito?
eh fee-NEE-toh?

How much do I owe you?
Quanto le devo?
KWAHN-toh leh DEH-vo?

🦁 21. Problems and Police

Although the situations suggested below may never happen to you, the words are useful to know, just in case.

Go away!
Vada via!
VA-da VEE-ya!

Leave me alone!
Mi lasci in pace!
mee LA-shee een PA-cheh!

I'll call a policeman.
Chiamo la polizia.
K'YA-mo la po-leet-SEE-ya.

Police!
Guardia!
GWAHRD-ya!

Help!
Aiuto!
ah-YOO-toh!

What's going on?
Cosa succede?
KO-za soot-CHEH-deh?

This person is annoying me.
Questa persona non mi lascia in pace.
KWESS-ta pair-so-na nohn mee LA-sha een PA-cheh.

Where is the police station?
Dov'è la stazione di polizia?
doh-VEH la stahts-YO-neh dee po-leet-SEE-ya.

I have been robbed of ...
Mi hanno rubato ...
mee AHN-no roo-BA-toh ...

... my wallet.
... il portafoglio.
eel por-ta-FOHL-yo.

... my watch.
... l'orologio.
lo-ro-LO-jo.

... jewelry.
... i gioielli.
... ee joy-YEL-lee.

... my suitcase.
... la valigia.
... la va-LEE-ja.

... my car.
... la macchina.
... la MAHK-kee-na.

Stop that man!
Fermate quell'uomo!
fair-MA-teh
  kwel-LWO-mo!

He's the thief.
È lui il ladro.
eh lwee eel LA-dro.

**Do you wish to make a
  complaint?**
Vuole presentare querela?
*VWO-leh preh-zen-TA-reh
  kweh-REH-la?*

Wait!
Aspetti!
ah-SPET-tee!

I am innocent.
Sono innocente.
SO-no een-no-CHEN-teh.

I haven't done anything.
Non ho fatto niente.
*nohn oh FAHT-toh
  N'YEN-teh.*

I don't recognize him.
Non lo riconosco.
nohn lo ree-ko-NOHS-ko.

I need a lawyer.
Voglio un avvocato.
*VOHL-yo oon
  ahv-vo-KA-toh.*

Notify the American Consul.
Notifichi il console americano.
no-TEE-fee-kee eel KOHN-so-leh ah-meh-ree-KA-no.

It's nothing.
Non è niente.
nohn eh N'YEN-teh.

It's a misunderstanding.
È un malinteso.
eh oon ma-leen-TEH-zo.

Don't worry.
Non si preoccupi.
*nohn see preh-OHK-
  koo-pee.*

Can I go now?
Posso andare ora?
*POHS-so ahn-DA-reh
  OH-ra?*

🦁 22. Housekeeping

The following chapter will be especially interesting for those who plan to stay longer in Italy or have occasion to employ Italian-speaking baby sitters or household help, abroad or even at home.

What is your name?
Come si chiama?
KO-meh see K'YA-ma?

Where did you work before?
Dove ha lavòrato prima?
DOH-veh ah la-vo-RA-toh PREE-ma?

Can you take care of a baby?
È capace di curare un bambino?
eh ka-PA-cheh dee koo-RA-reh oon bahm-BEE-no?

Can you cook?
Pùo cucinare?
pwo koo-chee-NA-reh?

We will pay you ——— lire per week.
La pagheremo ——— lire ogni settimana.
la pa-ghch-REH-mo ——— lee-reh OHN-yee set-tee-MA-na.

Thursday will be your day off.
Giovedì è il suo giorno di libertà.
jo-veh-DEE eh eel SOO-wo JOR-no dee lee-bair-TA.

This is your room.
Questa è la sua stanza.
KWESS-ta eh la SOO-wa STAHNT-sa.

Please clean . . .
Per favore pulisca . . .
pair fa-VO-reh
poo-LEES-ka . . .

. . . the living room.
. . . la sala di soggiorno.
. . . la SA-la dee
sohd-JOR-no.

. . . the dining room.
. . . la sala da pranzo.
. . . la SA-la da
PRAHNT-so.

. . . the bedroom.
. . . la stanza da letto.
. . . la STAHNT-sa da
LET-toh.

. . . the bathroom.
. . . il bagno.
. . . eel BAHN-yo.

. . . the kitchen.
. . . la cucina.
. . . la koo-CHEE-na.

Wash the dishes.
Lavi i piatti.
LA-vee ee P'YAHT-tee.

Sweep the floor.
Scopi il pavimento.
SKO-pee eel
pa-vee-MEN-toh.

Use the vacuum cleaner.
Usi l'aspirapolvere.
OO-zee la-spee-ra-POHL-
veh-reh.

. . . the broom.
. . . la scopa.
. . . la SKO-pa.

Polish the silver.
Lucidi l'argenteria.
LOO-chee-dee lar-jen-teh-REE-ya.

Make the beds.
Faccia i letti.
FAHT-cha ee LET-tee.

Change the sheets.
Cambi le lenzuola.
KAHM-bee leh
lend-ZWO-la.

Wash this.
Lavi questo.
LA-vee KWESS-toh.

Iron this.
Stiri questo.
STEE-ree KWESS-toh.

Have you finished?
Ha finito?
ah fee-NEE-toh?

What do you need?
Di che cosa ha bisogno?
dee keh KO-za ah bee-ZOHN-yo?

Go to the market.
Vada al mercato.
VA-da ahl mair-KA-toh.

Here is the list.
Ecco la lista.
EHK-ko la LEES-ta.

Put the milk in the refrigerator.
Metta il latte nel frigorifero.
MET-ta eel LAHT-tch nel free-go-REE-feh-ro.

If someone calls, write the name here.
Se qualcuno chiama, scriva il nome qui.
seh kwahl-KOO-no K'YA-ma, SKREE-va eel NO-meh kwee.

I'll be at this number.
Sarò a questo numero.
sa-RO ah KWESS-toh NOO-meh-ro.

I'll be back at 4 o'clock.
Tornerò alle quattro.
tor-neh-RO AHL-leh KWAHT-tro.

Feed the baby at ———— o'clock.
Dia da mangiare al bambino alle ————.
DEE-ya da mahn-JA-reh ahl bahm-BEE-no AHL-leh ————.

Give the child a bath.
Faccia il bagno al bambino.
FAHT-cha eel BAHN-yo ahl bahm-BEE-no.

Put him to bed at eight.
Lo metta a letto alle otto.
lo MET-ta ah LET-toh AHL-leh OHT-toh.

Serve lunch at 2 o'clock.
Serva la colazione alle due.
SAIR-va la ko-lahts-YO-neh AHL-leh DOO-weh.

Did anyone telephone?
Ha telefonato qualcuno?
ah teh-leh-fo-NA-toh kwahl-KOO-no?

We are having guests for dinner.
Abbiamo ospiti a pranzo.
ahb-B'YA-mo OH-spee-tee ah PRAHNT-so.

Serve dinner at 9 o'clock.
Serva il pranzo alle nove.
SAIR-va eel PRAHNT-so AHL-leh NO-veh.

🦁 23. A New Type of Dictionary

The following dictionary gives a list of English words with their translation into Italian to enable you to make up your own sentences in addition to those given in the phrase book. By using these words together with the following advice and short cuts, you will be able to make up hundreds of sentences by yourself. Only one Italian equivalent is given for each English word—the one most immediately useful to you—so that you won't be in any doubt about which word to use. Every word in the dictionary is followed by its phonetic pronunciation, so you will have no trouble being understood.

All Italian nouns are either masculine or feminine. If a noun ends in -o, it is usually masculine; if it ends in -a, it is usually feminine. The gender of any exceptions to this rule and of nouns ending in -e or any other letter is noted by an "(m)" or "(f)" after the noun in the dictionary.

Adjectives usually come after their nouns. All adjectives in this dictionary are given in the masculine form only. An adjective that ends in -o must change its ending to -a when it goes with a feminine noun:

> **il cappello nuovo**   the new hat
> (Il is the masculine form for "the.")
> **la casa nuova**   the new house
> (La is the feminine form for "the.")

Adjectives that end in -e are the same for both masculine and feminine:

> **il cappello grande**   the big hat
> **la casa grande**   the big house

(The word for "the" becomes l' before either masculine or feminine nouns beginning with a vowel: l'uomo—the man. And it becomes lo before masculine nouns beginning with

s followed by another consonant or with z: **lo specchio—**
the mirror.)

Nouns and adjectives that end in **-o** or **-e** form their
plurals by changing the ending to **-i.** Those that end in **-a**
form the plural by changing **-a** to **-e:**

> **i cappelli nuovi (grandi)** the new (big) hats
> (I is the masculine plural form for "the.")
> **le case nuove (grandi)** the new (big) houses
> (Le is the feminine plural form for "the.")

(The word for "the" becomes **gli** in the plural before
masculine nouns beginning either with a vowel, with s followed by another consonant, or with z: **gli uomini—**the
men; **gli specchi—**the mirrors.)

The verbs in the dictionary are given in the infinitive
form. In actual use, their endings change according to the
subject. Although a full grammatical explanation is not
within the scope of this book, the following table will help
you to use and recognize the present-tense forms of most
of the verbs in the dictionary. These are very important
because the subject pronouns—"I," "you," "he," "she,"
etc.—are frequently dropped and only the *ending* of the
verb indicates the person referred to.

Verbs are divided into three groups according to their
infinitive endings **-are, -ere,** and **-ire. Parlare** (to speak),
vendere (to sell), and **partire** (to leave) are examples of the
first, second, and third groups. Each verb has six forms in
each tense, depending on what person or persons is referred to. Here is the present tense of **parlare** (to speak)
with its English equivalents:

(io) parlo	I speak, I am speaking
(tu) parli	you (familiar) speak, you are speaking
(Lei, egli, ella) parla	you (formal) speak, you are speaking; he, she speaks; he, she is speaking

(noi) parliamo	we speak, we are speaking
(voi) parlate	you (plural) speak, you are speaking
(Loro, essi, esse) parlano	you (plural, formal), they (m or f) speak; you, they are speaking

The six forms for the present tense of **vendere** and **partire** are:

> **vendo, vendi, vende, vendiamo, vendete, vendono**
> **parto, parti, parte, partiamo, partite, partono**

There is another group of verbs ending in **-ire** which form their present tense like **capire** (to understand):

> **capisco, capisci, capisce, capiamo, capite, capiscono**

Many important verbs are somewhat irregular in their forms. These appear in different sections of the phrase book in the forms most useful for you to know and use. In addition, in order to help you make your own sentences, the present tense of "to be," "to go," "to come," "to have," and "to want" are given within the dictionary.

We put the Italian pronouns above in parentheses to remind you that they are often dropped in conversation, as the verb *ending* is what is important. We have not indicated a pronoun for "it" because in Italian everything is masculine or feminine and therefore "it" is "he" or "she."

Tu, Lei, voi, and **Loro** all mean "you." However *you* should use the polite form **Lei** when speaking to one person and **Loro** when speaking to more than one. The familiar forms **tu** and **voi** are commonly used within the family, between close friends, among students, and to children.

You can do a lot of communicating by using simply the present tense. But, in addition, you can use the infinitive to express a variety of other concepts. To say something must be done or is necessary, use **è necessario** directly with the infinitive:

It is necessary to leave. È necessario partire.

To say you want to do something or to invite someone to do something, use the appropriate form of "to want" with the infinitive of the second verb:

> I want to go. Voglio andare.
> Do you want to go? Vuole andare?

For the negative, use non in front of the verb:

> I don't want to go. Non voglio andare.

To give a polite command, add -i to the stem of the first conjugation, and -a for the other two:

> Speak! Parli!
> Leave! Parta!

For basic conversational purposes the present tense of "to go"—andare—can indicate the future according to the context: "Next year, we're going to Italy"—L'anno prossimo, andiamo in Italia.

Although the Italian present tense of verbs is equivalent to both the English simple present tense and the present progressive tense, you can also use the Italian present participle with the present tense form of stare (to be), exactly like the English progressive. The present participle ends in -ando for a verb whose infinitive ends in -are, and in -endo for a verb whose infinitive ends in -ere or -ire:

> I am eating. Sto mangiando.

To form the conversational past or perfect tense, use the present tense of avere (to have) or essere (to be) with the past participle of the verb. The past participles of verbs of the first group end in -ato; those of the second group end in -uto, -eso, or -esso; and those of the third in -ito. Some important past participles that are formed irregularly are listed in the dictionary. Most verbs use avere to form the past tense:

I gave, I have given	ho dato
we received, we have received	abbiamo ricevuto
you finished, you have finished	ha finito

Verbs that use "to be"—essere—to make the past tense are usually those of coming, going, arriving, leaving, etc.:

| I left, I have left | Sono partito |
| he arrived, he has arrived | È arrivato |

The past participle used with essere is like an adjective in that it agrees with the subject. A woman would say: Sono partita—I left.

Italian is fond of contractions: "To the"—a in combination with the definite article il, lo, la, l', i, gli, or le—becomes al, allo, alla, all', ai, agli, or alle respectively. "Of the"—di plus il, lo, la, l' i, gli, or le—becomes del, dello, della, dell', dei, degli, or delle; these forms are also used to mean "some" or "any."

The ubiquitous little words ci and ne take the place of the combinations of a and di respectively with another word when that word has already been referred to. Ci stands for the combination of a with the definite article and a noun and means "to it," "to them," or "there"; ne stands for the combination of di with the definite article and a noun and means "of it," of them," "some," or "any":

| She's going there. | Ci va. |
| I want two of them. | Ne voglio due. |

The possessive of nouns is always expressed by di:

| Robert's house | la casa di Roberto |

The possessive pronouns are listed individually in the dictionary. Observe that these pronouns agree in gender and number with the noun they refer to (not with the gender of the person possessing as in English):

| my hat and his (hers) | il mio cappello ed il suo |
| my house and his (hers) | la mia casa e la sua |

Object pronouns are given alphabetically within the dictionary. In sentences they are generally placed before the verb:

Tell me. **Mi dica.**
Don't tell her anything. **Non le dica niente.**
She gives him the check. **Ella gli da l'assegno.**

With this advice and the indications given in the dictionary, you will be able to use this communicating dictionary to make up countless sentences on your own and to converse with anyone you may meet.

There is, of course, much more to Italian grammar than these few suggestions we have given you—for example, the other moods and tenses, irregularities of the Italian verb, the different types of pronouns, the diminutives of nouns, and the numerous idioms and sayings that reflect the wisdom, poetry, and history of Italian culture. But you can effectively use this selected basic vocabulary as an important step, or even springboard, to enter the wonderful world that is the Italian heritage and, by practice, absorb and constantly improve your command of this melodious and beautiful language.

A

a, an	un, uno (m)	*oon, OO-no,*
	una (f)	*OO-na,*
	un (m or f)	*oon*
absent	assente	*ahs-SEN-teh*
about (concerning)	a proposito di	*ah pro-PO-zee-toh dee*
above	sopra	*SO-pra*
(to) accept	accettare	*aht-chet-TA-reh*
accident	incidente	*een-chee-DEN-teh*
account	conto	*KOHN-toh*
across	attraverso	*aht-tra-VAIR-so*
act	atto	*AHT-toh*
actor	attore	*aht-TOH-reh*
actress	attrice	*aht-TREE-cheh*
address	indirizzo	*een-dee-REET-tso*
admission (price)	entrata	*en-TRA-ta*
advertisement	reclame (f)	*reh-KLA-meh*
advice	consiglio	*kohn-SEEL-yo*
(to be) afraid	aver paura	*ah-VAIR pa-OO-ra*
Africa	Africa	*AH-free-ka*
African	africano	*ah-free-KA-no*
after	dopo	*DOH-po*
afternoon	pomeriggio	*po-meh-REED-jo*
again	ancora	*ahn-KO-ra*

against	contro	*KOHN-tro*
age	età	*eh-TA*
agency	agenzia	*ah-jent-SEE-ya*
agent	agente (m)	*ah-JEN-teh*
ago	fa	*fa*

(See page 33 for use.)

(to) agree	essere d'accordo	*ES-seh-reh da-KOR-do*
ahead	avanti	*ah-VAHN-tee*
air	aria	*AHR-ya*
air conditioned	aria condizionata	*AHR-ya kohn-deets-yo-NA-ta*
air force	aeronautica	*ah-eh-ro-NOW-tee-ka*
(by) air mail	via aerea	*VEE-ah ah-EH-reh-ah*
airplane	aereo	*ah-EH-reh-oh*
airport	aereoporto	*ah-eh-reh-oh-POR-toh*
all	tutto	*TOOT-toh*
That's all!	È tutto!	*eh TOOT-toh!*
allow	permettere	*pair-MET-teh-reh*
all right	va bene	*va BEH-neh*
almost	quasi	*KWA-zee*
alone	solo	*SO-lo*
already	già	*ja*
also	anche	*AHN-keh*
always	sempre	*SEM-preh*

(I) am	sono	*SO-no*

(Used with the present participle. See introduction to the dictionary.)

	sto	*sto*
America	America	*ah-MEH ree-ka*
American	americano	*ah-meh-ree-KA-no*
amusing	divertente	*dee-vehr-TEN-teh*
and	e, ed (before a vowel)	*eh, ed*
angry	arrabbiato	*ar-rahb-B'YA-toh*
animal	animale (m)	*ah-nee-MA-leh*
ankle	caviglia	*ka-VEEL-ya*
annoying	noioso	*no-YO-so*
another	un altro	*oon AHL-tro*
answer	risposta	*rees-PO-sta*
antiseptic	antisettico	*ahn-tee-SET-tee-ko*
any	ne	*neh*

(See introduction to the dictionary.)

anyone	qualsiasi persona	*kwahl-SEE-ah-see pair-SO-na*
anything	qualsiasi cosa	*kwahl-SEE-ah-see KO-za*
anywhere	qualsiasi posto	*kwahl-SEE-ah-see PO-sto*
apartment	appartamento	*ahp-par-ta-MEN-toh*
apple	mela	*MEH-la*
appointment	appuntamento	*ahp-poon-ta-MEN-toh*

April	aprile	*ah-PREE-leh*
Arab, Arabic	arabo	*AH-ra-bo*
architecture	architettura	*ar-kee-tet-TOO-ra*
are		
you (sg) are	Lei è	*lay eh*
we are	siamo	*S'YA-mo*
you (pl) are	Loro sono	*LO-ro SO-no*
they are	sono	*SO-no*
there are	ci sono	*chee SO-no*

(The following forms are used with the present participle. See introduction to the dictionary.)

you (sg) are	Lei sta	*lay sta*
we are	stiamo	*ST'YA-mo*
you (pl) are	Loro stanno	*LO-ro STAHN-no*
they are	stanno	*STAHN-no*
arm	braccio	*BRAHT-cho*
army	esercito	*eh-ZAIR-chee-toh*
around (surrounding)	intorno	*een-TOR-no*
around (approximately)	circa	*CHEER-ka*
(to) arrive	arrivare	*ar-ree-VA-reh*
art	arte (f)	*AR-teh*
artist	artista (m)	*ar-TEES-ta*
as	come	*KO-meh*
Asia	Asia	*AHS-ya*

(to) ask	domandare	*doh-mahn-DA-reh*
asleep	addormentato	*ahd-dor-men-TA-toh*
asparagus	asparagi (m pl)	*ahs-PA-ra-jee*
aspirin	aspirina	*ahs-pee-REE-na*
ass	asino	*AH-see-no*
at (location)	a, in	*ah, een*
at (time)	alle	*AHL-leh*
Atlantic	Atlantico	*aht-LAHN-tee-ko*
atomic	atomico	*ah-TOH-mee-ko*
August	agosto	*ah-GOHS-toh*
aunt	zia	*DZEE-ah*
Australia	Australia	*ows-TRAHL-ya*
Australian	australiano	*ows-trahl-YA-no*
Austria	Austria	*OWS-tr'ya*
Austrian	austriaco	*ows-TREE-ah-ko*
author	autore (m)	*ow-TOH-reh*
automatic	automatico	*ow-toh-MA-tee-ko*
automobile	automobile (f)	*ow-toh-MO-bee-leh*
autumn	autunno	*ow-TOON-no*
(to) avoid	evitare	*eh-vee-TA-reh*
away	via	*VEE-ah*

B

| baby | bebè (m) | *beh-BEH* |

bachelor	scapolo	*SKA-po-lo*
back (part of body)	schiena	*SK'YEH-na*
bad	cattivo	*kaht-TEE-vo*
baggage	bagaglio	*ba-GAHL-yo*
balcony (theater)	balconata	*bahl-ko-NA-ta*
banana	banana	*ba-NA-na*
bandage	benda	*BEN-da*
bank	banca	*BAHN-ka*
bar	bar	*bar*
barber	barbiere (m)	*bar-B'YEH-reh*
baritone	baritono	*ba-REE-toh-no*
basso	basso	*BAHS-so*
bath	bagno	*BAHN-yo*
bathing suit	costume da bagno	*kohs-TOO-meh da BAHN-yo*
bathroom	stanza da bagno	*STAHNT-sa da BAHN-yo*
battery	batteria	*baht-teh-REE-ya*
battle	battaglia	*baht-TAHL-ya*
(to) be	essere	*EHS-seh-reh*

(See also "am," "is," "are," "was," "were," "been.")

beach	spiaggia	*SP'YAHD-ja*
beans	fagioli (m pl)	*fa-JO-lee*
beard	barba	*BAR-ba*
beautiful	bello	*BEL-lo*

beauty	bellezza	*bel-LET-tsa*
beauty shop	salone di bellezza	*sa-LO-neh dee bel-LET-tsa*
because	perchè	*pair-KEH*
bed	letto	*LET-toh*
bedroom	stanza da letto	*STAHNT-sa da LET-toh*
beef	manzo	*MAHNT-so*
been	stato	*STA-toh*
beer	birra	*BEER-ra*
before	prima	*PREE-ma*
(to) begin	cominciare	*ko-meen-CHA-reh*
behind	dietro	*D'YEH-tro*
(to) believe	credere	*KREH-deh-reh*
belt	cintura	*cheen-TOO-ra*
beside	vicino a	*vee-CHEE-no ah*
best (adj)	il migliore	*eel meel-YO-reh*
better	meglio	*MAIL-yo*
between	tra	*tra*
bicycle	bicicletta	*bee-chee-CLET-ta*
big	grande	*GRAHN-deh*
bill	conto	*KOHN-toh*
bird	uccello	*oot-CHEL-lo*
birthday	compleanno	*kohm-pleh-AHN-no*
black	nero	*NEH-ro*

blond	biondo	B'YOHN-doh
blood	sangue (m)	SAHN-gweh
blouse	blusa	BLOO-za
blue	blu	bloo
boardinghouse	pensione	pens-YO-neh
boat	barca	BAR-ka
body	corpo	KOR-po
book	libro	LEE-bro
bookstore	libreria.	lee-breh-REE-ya
born	nato	NA-toh
(to) borrow	imprestare	eem-pres-TA-reh
boss	padrone (m)	pa-DRO-neh
both	entrambi	en-TRAHM-bee
(to) bother	disturbare	dees-toor-BA-reh
bottle	bottiglia	boht-TEEL-ya
bottom	fondo	FOHN-doh
bought	comprato	kohm-PRA-toh
box (carton)	scatola	SKA-toh-la
box (theater)	palco	PAHL-ko
boy	ragazzo	ra-GAHT-tso
brain	cervello	chair-VEL-lo
brake	freno	FREH-no
brave	coraggioso	ko-rahd-JO-so
bread	pane (m)	PA-neh
(to) break	rompere	ROHM-peh-reh

breakfast	colazione (f)	ko-lahts-YO-neh
(to) breathe	respirare	res-pee-RA-reh
bridge	ponte (m)	POHN-teh
briefcase	cartella	kar-TEL-la
(to) bring	portare	por-TA-reh
Bring me . . .	Mi porti . . .	mee POR-tee
broken	rotto	ROHT-toh
brother	fratello	fra-TEL-lo
brother-in-law	cognato	kohn-YA-toh
brown	marrone	mar-RO-neh
brunette	bruna	BROO-na
(to) build	costruire	kohs-troo-EE-reh
building	edificio	eh-dee-FEE-cho
built	costruito	kohs-troo-EE-toh
bureau	burò	boo-RO
bus	autobus (m)	OW-toh-booss
business	affari (m pl)	ahf-FA-ree
business trip	viaggio d'affari	V'YAHD-jo dahf-FA-ree
bus stop	fermata dell'autobus	fair-MA-ta del-L'OW-toh-booss
busy	occupato	ohk-koo-PA-toh
but	ma	ma
butter	burro	BOOR-ro
button	bottone (m)	boht-TOH-neh

| (to) buy | comprare | *kohm-PRA-reh* |
| by | per | *pair* |

C

cabbage	cavolo	*KA-vo-lo*
cake	torta (f)	*TOR-ta*
(to) call	chiamare	*k'ya-MA-reh*
Call me.	Mi chiami.	*mee K'YA-mee.*
camera	macchina fotografica	*MAHK-kee-na fo-toh-GRA-fee-ka*
can (to be able)	potere	*po-TEH-reh*
Can you . . . ?	Può Lei . . . ?	*pwo lay . . . ?*
I can	posso	*POHS-so*
I can't	non posso	*nohn POHS-so*
can (container)	scatola di latta	*SKA-toh-la dee LAHT-ta*
canal	canale (m)	*ka-NA-leh*
can opener	apriscatole (m)	*ah-pree-SKA-toh-leh*
candy	caramella (f)	*ka-ra-MEL-la*
capable	capace	*ka-PA-cheh*
captain	capitano	*ka-pee-TA-no*
car	macchina	*MAHK-kee-na*
carburetor	carbura-tore (m)	*kar-boo-ra-TOH-reh*
card	carta	*KAR-ta*

careful	attento	*aht-TEN-toh*
(Be) careful!	Attenzione!	*aht-tents-YO-neh!*
careless	disattento	*dees-aht-TEN-toh*
carrot	carota	*ka-RO-ta*
(to) carry	portare	*por-TA-reh*
Carry this to . . .	Porti questo a . . .	*POR-tee KWES-toh ah . . .*
cashier	cassiere (m)	*kahs-S'YEH-reh*
castle	castello	*kahs-TEL-lo*
cat	gatto	*GAHT-toh*
cathedral	cattedrale (f)	*kaht-teh-DRA-leh*
Catholic	cattolico	*kaht-TOH-lee-ko*
celebration	celebrazione (f)	*cheh-leh-brahts-YO-neh*
cellar	cantina	*kahn-TEE-na*
cemetery	cimetero	*chee-meh-TEH-ro*
cent	centesimo	*chen-TEH-see-mo*
center	centro	*CHEN-tro*
century	secolo	*SEH-ko-lo*
certainly	certamente	*chair-ta-MEN-teh*
certificate of origin	certificato d'origine	*chair-tee-fee-KA-toh doh-REE-jee-neh*
chair	sedia	*SAY-d'ya*
change	cambiamento	*kahm-b'ya-MEN-toh*
(to) change	cambiare	*kahm-B'YA-reh*

charming	affascinante	*ahf-fah-shee-NAHN-teh*
chauffeur	autista (m)	*ow-TEES-ta*
cheap	a buon mercato	*ah bwohn mair-KA-toh*
check	assegno	*ahs-SEN-yo*
checkroom	guardaroba	*gwar-da-RO-ba*
cheese	formaggio	*for-MAHD-jo*
cherries	ciliege (f pl)	*cheel-YEH-jeh*
chest	petto	*PET-toh*
chicken	pollo	*POHL-lo*
child	bambino	*bahm-BEE-no*
chin	mento	*MEN-toh*
China	Cina	*CHEE-na*
Chinese	cinese	*chee-NEH-zeh*
chocolate	cioccolata	*chohk-ko-LA-ta*
chop	costoletta	*kohs-toh-LET-ta*
church	chiesa	*K'YEH-za*
cigar	sigaro	*SEE-ga-ro*
cigarette	sigaretta	*see-ga-RET-ta*
city	città	*cheet-TA*
(to) clean	pulire	*poo-LEE-reh*
clear	chiaro	*K'YA-ro*
clever	intelligente	*een-tel-lee-JEN-teh*
climate	clima	*KLEE-ma*
close (near)	vicino	*vee-CHEE-no*

(to) close	chiudere	*K'YOO-deh-reh*
closed	chiuso	*K'YOO-zo*
clothes	vestiti (m pl)	*ves-TEE-tee*
coast	costa	*KOHS-ta*
coat	cappotto	*kahp-POHT-toh*
coffee	caffè (m)	*kahf-FEH*
coin	moneta	*mo-NEH-ta*
cold	freddo	*FRED-doh*
college	università	*oo-nee-ver-see-TA*
colonel	colonnello	*ko-lohn-NEL-lo*
color	colore (m)	*ko-LO-reh*
comb	pettine (m)	*PET-tee-neh*
(to) come	venire	*veh-NEE-reh*
I come	vengo	*VEN-go*
you (sg) come	Lei viene	*lay V'YEH-neh*
he, she comes	viene	*V'YEH-neh*
we come	veniamo	*ven-YA-mo*
you (pl) come	Loro vengono	*LO-ro VEN-go-no*
they come	vengono	*VEN-go-no*
Come!	Venga!	*VEN-ga!*
Come in!	Avanti!	*ah-VAHN-tee!*
(to) come back	ritornare	*ree-tor-NA-reh*
company	compagnia	*kohm-pahn-YEE-ah*
competition	competi-zione (f)	*kohm-peh-teets-YO-neh*

complete	completo	*kohm-PLEH-toh*
computer	calcolatore (m)	*kahl-ko-la-TOH-reh*
concert	concerto	*kohn-CHAIR-toh*
conductor	conduttore (m)	*kohn-doot-TOH-reh*
congratulations	congratu- lazioni (f pl)	*kohn-gra-too-lahts- YO-nee*
(to) continue	continuare	*kohn-tee-NWA-reh*
conversation	conversa- zione (f)	*kohn-ver-sahts- YO-neh*
cook	cuoco (m), cuoca (f)	*KWO-ko, KWO-ka*
(to) cook	cucinare	*koo-chee-NA-reh*
cool	fresco	*FRES-ko*
copy	copia	*KOHP-ya*
corkscrew	cavatappi (m)	*ka-va-TAHP-pee*
corner	angolo	*AHN-go-lo*
correct	esatto	*eh-ZAHT-toh*
(to) cost	costare	*kohs-TA-reh*
cotton	cotone (m)	*ko-TOH-neh*
cough	tosse (f)	*TOS-seh*
country	paese (m)	*pa-EH-zeh*
cousin	cugino	*koo-JEE-no*
cow	mucca	*MOOK-ka*
crab	granchio	*GRAHNK-yo*
crazy	matto	*MAHT-toh*
(to) crate	imballare	*eem-bahl-LA-reh*

cream	crema	*KREH-ma*
(to) cross	incrociare	*een-kro-CHA-reh*
crossing	incrocio	*een-KRO-cho*
cup	tazza	*TAHT-tsa*
custom (habit)	usanza	*oo-SAHNT-sa*
customs form	formulario di dogana	*for-moo-LAR-yo dee doh-GA-na*
customs office	ufficio di dogana	*oof-FEE-cho dee doh-GA-na*
(to) cut	tagliare	*tahl-YA-reh*

D

(to) dance	ballare	*bahl-LA-reh*
dangerous	pericoloso	*peh-ree-ko-LO-zo*
dark	scuro	*SKOO-ro*
darling	tesoro	*teh-ZO-ro*
date (day)	data	*DA-ta*
date (appointment)	appuntamento	*ahp-poon-ta-MEN-toh*
daughter	figlia	*FEEL-ya*
daughter-in-law	nuora	*NWO-ra*
day	giorno	*JOR-no*
dead	morto	*MOR-toh*
dear	caro	*KA-ro*
December	dicembre	*dee-CHEM-breh*

(to) decide	decidere	*deh-CHEE-deh-reh*
deep	profondo	*pro-FOHN-doh*
delay	ritardo	*ree-TAR-doh*
delicious	delizioso	*deh-leets-YO-zo*
delighted	contento	*kohn-TEN-toh*
dentist	dentista (m)	*den-TEES-ta*
department store	grande magazzino	*GRAHN-deh ma-gahd-DZEE-no*
desk	scrivania	*skree-va-NEE-ya*
detour	deviazione (f)	*dev-yahts-YO-neh*
devil	diavolo	*D'YA-vo-lo*
dictionary	dizionario	*deets-yo-NAHR-yo*
different	differente	*deef-feh-REN-teh*
difficult	difficile	*deef-FEE-chee-leh*
(to) dine	pranzare	*prahnt-SA-reh*
dining room	sala da pranzo	*SA-la da PRAHNT-so*
dinner	pranzo	*PRAHNT-so*
direction	direzione (f)	*dee-rets-YO-neh*
dirty	sporco	*SPOR-ko*
disappointed	dispiaciuto	*dees-p'ya-CHOO-toh*
discount	sconto	*SKOHN-toh*
divorced	divorziato	*dee-vorts-YA-toh*
(to) do	fare	*FA-reh*

"Do" is not used to ask a question or to form the negative. For a question, simply put the subject after the verb; and for the negative, use **non** before the verb:

Do you want . . . ?	Vuole Lei . . . ?	*VWO-leh lay . . . ?*
I don't understand.	Non capisco.	*nohn ka-PEES-ko.*
Don't do that!	Non faccia così!	*nohn FAHT-cha ko-ZEE!*
dock	molo	*MO-lo*
doctor	dottore (m)	*doht-TOH-reh*
dog	cane (m)	*KA-neh*
dollar	dollaro	*DOHL-la-ro*
door	porta	*POR-ta*
down	giù	*joo*
downtown	al centro	*ahl CHEN-tro*
dress	vestito	*ves-TEE-toh*
(to) drink	bere	*BEH-reh*
(to) drive	guidare	*gwee-DA-reh*
driver	autista (m)	*ow-TEES-ta*
driver's license	patente (f)	*pa-TEN-teh*
drugstore	farmacia	*far-ma-CHEE-ya*
drunk	ubriaco	*oo-bree-AH-ko*
dry cleaner	pulitore a secco (m)	*poo-lee-TOH-reh ah SEK-ko*
duck	anitra	*AH-nee-tra*

E

| each | ognuno | *ohn-YOO-no* |

ear	orecchio	*oh-REK-k'yo*
early	presto	*PRES-toh*
(to) earn	guadagnare	*gwa-dahn-YA-reh*
earth	terra	*TAIR-ra*
east	est (m)	*est*
easy	facile	*FA-chee-leh*
(to) eat	mangiare	*mahn-JA-reh*
eggs	uova (f pl)	*WO-va*
eight	otto	*OHT-toh*
eighteen	diciotto	*dee-CHOHT-toh*
eighty	ottanta	*oht-TAHN-ta*
either (one)	l'uno o l'altro	*LOO-no oh LAHL-tro*
either . . . or	o . . . o	*oh . . . oh*
elbow	gomito	*GO-mee-toh*
electric	elettrico	*eh-LET-tree-ko*
elephant	elefante (m)	*eh-leh-FAHN-teh*
elevator	ascensore (m)	*ah-shen-SO-reh*
embassy	ambasciata	*ahm-ba-SHA-ta*
emergency	emergenza	*eh-mair-JENT-sa*
(to) employ	impiegare	*eem-p'yeh-GA-reh*
employee	impiegato	*eem-p'yeh-GA-toh*
end	fine (f)	*FEE-neh*
(to) end	finire	*fee-NEE-reh*
England	Inghilterra	*een-gheel-TAIR-ra*
English	inglese	*een-GLEH-zeh*

entertaining	divertente	*dee-vair-TEN-teh*
error	errore (m)	*air-RO-reh*
especially	specialmente	*speh-chahl-MEN-teh*
Europe	Europa	*eh-oo-RO-pa*
European	europeo	*eh-oo-ro-PEH-oh*
even	perfino	*pair-FEE-no*
evening	sera	*SEH-ra*
ever (sometime)	mai	*my*
every	ogni	*OHN-yee*
everybody	tutti	*TOOT-tee*
everything	tutto	*TOOT-toh*
exactly	esattamente	*eh-zaht-ta-MEN-teh*
excellent	eccellente	*et-chel-LEN-teh*
except	eccetto	*et-CHET-toh*
(to) exchange	cambiare	*kahm-B'YA-reh*
Excuse me!	Mi scusi!	*mee SKOO-zeel*
exit	uscita	*oo-SHEE-ta*
expensive	costoso	*ko-STO-zo*
experience	esperienza	*es-pair-YENT-sa*
explanation	spiegazione (f)	*sp'yeh-gahts-YO-neh*
(to) export	esportare	*es-por-TA-reh*
extra	extra	*EX-tra*
eye	occhio	*OHK-k'yo*

F

face	faccia	*FAHT-cha*
fair (exposition)	fiera	*F'YEH-ra*
factory	fabbrica	*FAHB-bree-ka*
fall (autumn)	autunno	*ow-TOON-no*
(to) fall	cadere	*ka-DEH-reh*
family	famiglia	*fa-MEEL-ya*
famous	famoso	*fa-MO-zo*
far	lontano	*lohn-TA-no*
How far?	Quanto è lontano?	*KWAHN-toh eh lohn-TA-no?*
farm	fattoria	*faht-toh-REE-ya*
farther	più lontano	*p'yoo lohn-TA-no*
fast	veloce	*veh-LO-cheh*
fat	grasso	*GRAHS-so*
father	padre (m)	*PA-dreh*
February	febbraio	*feb-BRA-yo*
(to) feel	sentire	*sen-TEE-reh*
fever	febbre (f)	*FEB-breh*
few	pochi	*PO-kee*
fifteen	quindici	*KWEEN-dee-chee*
fifty	cinquanta	*cheen-KWAHN-ta*
(to) fight	combattere	*kohm-BAHT-teh-reh*
(to) fill	riempire	*r'yem-PEE-reh*

film (movie)	film (m)	*feelm*
film (for camera)	pellicola	*pel-LEE-ko-la*
finally	finalmente	*fee-nahl-MEN-teh*
(to) find	trovare	*tro-VA-reh*
(to) find out	scoprire	*sko-PREE-reh*
finger	dito	*DEE-toh*
(to) finish	finire	*fee-NEE-reh*
finished	finito	*fee-NEE-toh*
fire	fuoco	*FWO-ko*
first	primo	*PREE-mo*
fish	pesce (m)	*PEH-sheh*
(to) fish	pescare	*pess-KA-reh*
five	cinque	*CHEEN-kweh*
flight	volo	*VU-lo*
floor	pavimento	*pa-vee-MEN-toh*
flower	fiore (m)	*F'YO-reh*
fly (insect)	mosca	*MO-ska*
(to) fly	volare	*vo-LA-reh*
food	cibo	*CHEE-bo*
foot	piede (m)	*P'YEH-deh*
for	per	*pair*
foreigner	straniero	*strahn-YEH-ro*
forest	foresta	*fo-RESS-ta*
(to) forget	dimenticare	*dee-men-tee-KA-reh*

Don't forget!	Non si dimen-	*nohn see dee-MEN-*
	tichi!	*tee-kee!*
fork	forchetta	*for-KET-ta*
forty	quaranta	*kwa-RAHN-ta*
fountain	fontana	*fohn-TA-na*
four	quattro	*KWAHT-tro*
fourteen	quattordici	*kwaht-TOR-dee-chee*
fox	volpe (f)	*VOHL-peh*
France	Francia	*FRAHN-cha*
free	libero	*LEE-beh-ro*
French	francese	*frahn-CHEH-zeh*
frequently	frequentemente	*freh-kwen-teh-MEN-teh*
fresh	fresco	*FRESS-ko*
Friday	venerdì	*ven-air-DEE*
fried	fritto	*FREET-toh*
friend	amico	*ah-MEE-ko*
frog	rana	*RA-na*
from	da	*da*
(in) front of	davanti a	*da-VAHN-tee. ah*
fruit	frutto	*FROOT-toh*
full	pieno	*P'YEH-no*
funny	buffo	*BOOF-fo*
furniture	mobili (m pl)	*MO-bee-lee*
future	futuro	*foo-TOO-ro*
in the future	nel futuro	*nel foo-TOO-ro*

G

game	gioco	*JO-ko*
garage	garage (m)	*ga-RAHZH*
garden	giardino	*jar-DEE-no*
gas	gas (m)	*gahss*
gas station	stazione di benzina (f)	*stahts-YO-neh dee bend-ZEE-na*
general (n or adj).	generale	*jen-eh-RA-leh*
gentleman	signore (m)	*seen-YO-reh*
German	tedesco	*teh-DESS-ko*
Germany	Germania	*jer-MAHN-ya*
(to) get (obtain)	ottenere	*oht-teh-NEH-reh*
(to) get (become)	diventare	*dee-ven-TA-reh*
(to) get off	scendere	*SHEN-deh-reh*
(to) get on	salire	*sa-LEE-reh*
(to) get out	uscire	*oo-SHEE-reh*
Get out!	Esca!	*ESS-ka!*
gift	regalo	*reh-GA-lo*
(to) give	dare	*DA-reh*
Give me . . .	Mi dia . . .	*mee DEE-ya . . .*
girl	ragazza	*ra-GAHT-tsa*
glass (for drinking)	bicchiere (m)	*beek-K'YEH-reh*

glass (for windows)	vetro	*VEH-tro*
(eye) glasses	occhiali (m pl)	*ohk-K'YA-lee*
glove	guanto	*GWAHN-toh*
(to) go	andare	*ahn-DA-reh*
I go	vado	*VA-doh*
you (sg) go	Lei va	*lay va*
he, she goes	va	*va*
we go	andiamo	*ahnd-YA-mo*
you (pl) go	Loro vanno	*LO-ro VAHN-no*
they go	vanno	*VAHN-no*
(to) go away	andare via	*ahn-DA-reh VEE-ya*
Go away!	Vada via!	*VA-da VEE-ya!*
(to) go back	ritornare	*ree-tor-NA-reh*
Go on!	Avanti!	*ah-VAHN-tee!*
goat	capra	*KA-pra*
God	Dio	*DEE-yo*
gold	oro	*OH-ro*
golf	golf (m)	*gohlf*
good	buono	*BWO-no*
Goodbye (formal)	ArrivederLa	*ahr-ree-veh-DAIR-la*
(less formal)	Arrivederci	*ahr-ree-veh-DAIR-chee*
(informal)	Ciao	*chow*
government	governo	*go-VAIR-no*

grandfather	nonno	*NOHN-no*
grandmother	nonna	*NOHN-na*
grapes	uva	*OO-va*
grateful	grato	*GRA-toh*
gray	grigio	*GREE-jo*
great	grande	*GRAHN-deh*
a great many	molti	*MOHL-tee*
Greece	Grecia	*GREH-cha*
Greek	greco	*GREH-ko*
green	verde	*VAIR-deh*
group	gruppo	*GROOP-po*
guide	guida	*GWEE-da*
guitar	chitarra	*kee-TAR-ra*

H

hair (m pl)	capelli	*ka-PEL-lee*
hairbrush	spazzola	*SPAHT-tso-la*
haircut	taglio di capelli	*TAHL-yo dee ka-PEL-lee*
half	metà	*meh-TA*
hand	mano (f)	*MA-no*
happy	felice	*feh-LEE-cheh*
hard	duro	*DOO-ro*
hat	cappello	*kahp-PEL-lo*

(to) have	avere	*ah-VEH-reh*
I have	ho	*oh*
you (sg) have	Lei ha	*lay ah*
he, she has	ha	*ah*
we have	abbiamo	*ahb-B'YA-mo*
you (pl) have	Loro hanno	*Lo-ro AHN-no*
they have	hanno	*AHN-no*
Have you?	Ha?	*ah?*
he	egli, lui	*EL-yee, LOO-ee*
head	testa	*TESS-ta*
(to) hear	sentire	*sen-TEE-reh*
heart	cuore (m)	*KWO-reh*
heavy	pesante	*peh-ZAHN-teh*
Hello!	Ciao!	*chow!*
(on the tele- phone)	Pronto!	*PROHN-toh!*
(to) help	aiutare	*ah-yoo-TA-reh*
Help!	Aiuto!	*ah-YOO-toh!*
her (pronoun)	la, le, lei	*la, leh, lay*
her (adj)	il suo, la sua, (pl) i suoi, le sue	*eel SOO-wo, la SOO- wa, ee swoy, leh SOO-eh*
here	qui	*kwee*
high	alto	*AHL-toh*
highway	autostrada	*ow-toh-STRA-da*

hill	collina	*kohl-LEE-na*
him	lo, gli, lui	*lo, l'yee, LOO-ee*
his	il suo, la sua, (pl) i suoi, le sue	*eel SOO-wo, la SOO-wa, ee swoy, leh SOO-oh*
history	storia	*STOR-ya*
home	casa	*KA-za*
at home	a casa	*ah KA-za*
horse	cavallo	*ka-VAHL-lo*
on horseback	a cavallo	*ah ka-VAHL-lo*
hospital	ospedale (m)	*ohs-peh-DA-leh*
hot	caldo	*KAHL-doh*
hotel	albergo	*ahl-BAIR-go*
hour	ora	*OH-ra*
house	casa	*KA-za*
how	come	*KO-meh*
however	in ogni caso	*een OHN-yee KA-zo*
hundred	cento	*CHEN-toh*
a hundred and one	centouno	*chen-toh-OO-no*
Hungary	Ungheria	*oon-geh-REE-ya*
Hungarian	ungherese	*oon-geh-REH-zeh*
(to be) hungry	aver fame	*ah-VAIR FA-meh*
(to) hunt	cacciare	*kaht-CHA-reh*
(to) hurry	sbrigarsi	*zbree-GAR-see*
Hurry up!	Presto!	*PRESS-toh!*

husband	marito	*ma-REE-toh*

I

I	io	*EE-yo*
ice	ghiaccio	*G'YAHT-cho*
ice cream	gelato	*jeh-LA-toh*
idiot	idiota	*eed-YO-ta*
if	se	*seh*
ill	ammalato	*ahm-ma-LA-toh*
(to) import	importare	*eem-por-TA-reh*
important	importante	*eem-por-TAHN-teh*
impossible	impossibile	*eem-pohs-SEE-bee-leh*
in	in	*een*
included	incluso	*een-KLOO-zo*
industry	industria	*een-DOOS-tr'ya*
information	informazione (f)	*een-for-mahts-YO-neh*
inhabitant	abitante (m)	*ah-bee-TAHN-teh*
inside	dentro	*DEN-tro*
instead	invece	*een-VEH-cheh*
intelligent	intelligente	*een-tel-lee-JEN-teh*
interested	interessato	*een-teh-res-SA-toh*
interesting	interessante	*een-teh-res-SAHN-teh*
interpreter	interprete (m)	*een-TAIR-preh-teh*

into	in	*een*
(to) introduce	presentare	*preh-zen-TA-reh*
invitation	invito	*een-VEE-toh*
is	è	*eh*

(Used with the present participle. See introduction to the dictionary.)

	sta	*sta*
island	isola	*EE-zo-la*
Israel	Israele	*eez-ra-YEH-leh*
Israeli	israeliano	*eez-ra-el-YA-no*
it (object)	lo, la	*lo, la*
its	il suo, la sua	*eel SOO-wo, la SOO-wa*
Italian	italiano	*ee-tahl-YA-no*
Italy	Italia	*ee-TAHL-ya*

J

jacket	giacca	*JAHK-ka*
jail	prigione (f)	*pree-JO-neh*
January	gennaio	*jen-NA-yo*
Japan	Giappone	*jahp-PO-neh*
Japanese	giapponese	*jahp-po-NEH-zeh*
jewelry	gioielli (m pl)	*joy-YEL-lee*
Jewish	ebreo	*eh-BREH-oh*
job	lavoro	*la-VO-ro*

joke	scherzo	*SKAIRT-so*
July	luglio	*LOOL-yo*
June	giugno	*JOON-yo*
just (only)	soltanto	*sohl-TAHN-toh*
just now	proprio adesso	*PROHP-r'yo ah-DESS-so*

K

(to) keep	tenere	*teh-NEH-reh*
Keep out!	Fuori!	*FWO-ree!*
Keep quiet!	Silenzio!	*see-LENTS-yo*
key	chiave (f)	*K'YA-veh*
kind (nice)	gentile	*jen-TEE-leh*
kind (type)	genere	*JEH-neh-reh*
king	re (m)	*reh*
kiss	bacio	*BA-cho*
kitchen	cucina	*koo-CHEE-na*
knee	ginocchio	*jee-NOHK-k'yo*
knife	coltello	*kohl-TEL-lo*
(to) know (a person)	conoscere	*ko-NO-sheh-reh*
(to) know (something)	sapere	*sa-PEH-reh*
Do you know . . . ?	Sa Lei . . . ?	*sa lay . . . ?*
Who knows?	Chi sa?	*kee sa?*

L

ladies' room	toeletta	*toh-eh-LET-ta*
lady	signora	*seen-YO-ra*
lake	lago	*LA-go*
lamb	agnello	*ahn-YEL-lo*
land	terra	*TAIR-ra*
language	lingua	*LEEN-gwa*
large	grande	*GRAHN-deh*
last	ultimo	*OOL-tee-mo*
late	tardi	*TAR-dee*
later	più tardi	*p'yoo TAR-dee*
law	legge (f)	*LED-jeh*
lawyer	avvocato	*ahv-vo-KA-toh*
(to) learn	imparare	*eem pa RA roh*
leather	cuoio	*KWO-yo*
(to) leave (something)	lasciare	*la-SHA-reh*
(to) leave (depart)	partire	*par-TEE-reh*
left	sinistro	*see-NEE-stro*
leg	gamba	*GAHM-ba*
lemon	limone (m)	*lee-MO-neh*
(to) lend	prestare	*press-TA-reh*
less (adv)	meno	*MEH-no*
lesson	lezione (f)	*lets-YO-neh*

Let's go!	Andiamo!	*ahnd-YA-mo!*
letter	lettera	*LET-teh-ra*
lettuce	lattuga	*laht-TOO-ga*
liberty	libertà	*lee-bair-TA*
lieutenant	luogotenente (m)	*lwo-go-teh-NEN-teh*
life	vita	*VEE-ta*
light (weight)	leggero	*led-JEH-ro*
light (illumination)	luce (f)	*LOO-cheh*
like (prep)	come	*KO-meh*
Like this.	Così.	*.ko-ZEE.*
(to) like	piacere	*p'ya-CHEH-reh*
linen	lino	*LEE-no*
lion	leone (m)	*leh-OH-neh*
lips	labbra (f pl)	*LAHB-bra*
the lips	le labbra	*leh LAHB-bra*
list	lista	*LEE-sta*
(to) listen	ascoltare	*ahs-kohl-TA-reh*
Listen!	Ascolti!	*ahs-KOHL-tee!*
little (small)	piccolo	*PEEK-ko-lo*
a little (of)	un poco (di)	*oon PO-ko (dee)*
(to) live	vivere	*VEE-veh-reh*
lived	vissuto	*vees-SOO-toh*
living room	salotto	*sa-LOHT-toh*
lobster	aragosta	*ah-ra-GO-sta*

long	lungo	*LOON-go*
(to) look	guardare	*gwahr-DA-reh*
Look!	Guardi!	*GWAHR-deel*
Look out!	Attenti!	*aht-TEN-tee!*
loose	sciolto	*SHOHL-toh*
(to) lose	perdere	*PAIR-deh-reh*
loss	perdita	*PAIR-dee-ta*
lost	perduto	*pair-DOO-toh*
lot (much)	molto	*MOHL-toh*
(to) love	amare	*ah-MA-reh*
low	basso	*BAHS-so*
luck	fortuna	*for-TOO-na*
Good luck!	Buona fortuna!	*BWO-na for-TOO-na!*
luggage	bagaglio	*ba-GAHL-yo*
lunch	seconda colazione (f)	*seh-KOHN-da ko-lahts-YO-neh*

M

machine	macchina	*MAHK-kee-na*
madam	signora	*seen-YO-ra*
made	fatto	*FAHT-toh*
maid	dome	*doh-MESS-tee-ka*
mailbox	buca p.	*BOO-ka DEL-la PO-sta*
(to) make	fare	*FA-reh*

man	uomo	*WO-mo*
men	uomini	*WO-mee-nee*
manager	amministra-tore (m)	*ahm-mee-nee-stra-TOH-reh*
many	molti	*MOHL-tee*
map	mappa	*MAHP-pa*
March (month)	marzo	*MART-so*
market	mercato	*mair-KA-toh*
married	sposato	*spo-ZA-toh*
Mass (religious)	messa	*MESS-sa*
matches	fiammiferi	*f'yahm-MEE-feh-ree*
May I?	Posso?	*POHS-so?*
May (month)	maggio	*MAHD-jo*
maybe	forse	*FOR-seh*
me	me, mi	*meh, mee*
(to) mean	voler dire	*vo-LAIR DEE-reh*
meat	carne (f)	*KAR-neh*
mechanic	meccanico	*mek-KA-nee-ko*
medicine	medicina	*meh-dee-CHEE-na*
Mediterranean	Mediterraneo	*meh-dee-tair-RA-neh-yo*
(to) meet (en-counter)	incontrare	*een-kohn-TRA-reh*
meeting	riunione (f)	*ree-oon-YO-neh*
member	membro	*MEM-bro*
(to) mend	accomodare	*ahk-ko-mo-DA-reh*

men's room	toeletta	*toh-eh-LET-ta*
menu	lista	*LEES-ta*
message	messaggio	*mehs-SAHD-jo*
meter	metro	*MEH-tro*
Mexico	Messico	*MEHS-see-ko*
(in the) middle	in mezzo	*een MEHD-dzo*
milk	latte (f)	*LAHT-teh*
million	milione (m)	*meel-YO-neh*
mine (See "my.")		
mineral water	aqua minerale (f)	*AH-kwa mee-neh-RA-leh*
minister	ministro	*mee-NEES-tro*
minute	minuto	*mee-NOO-toh*
Miss	signorina	*seen-yo-REE-na*
(to) miss (a train)	perdere	*PAIR-deh-reh*
(to) miss (someone)	sbagliare	*sbahl-YA-reh*
mistake	errore (m)	*air-RO-reh*
Mr.	signore	*seen-YO-reh*
Mrs.	signora	*seen-YO-ra*
misunderstanding	malinteso	*ma-leen-TEH-zo*
model	modello	*mo-DEL-lo*
modern	moderno	*mo-DAIR-no*
moment	momento	*mo-MEN-toh*

Monday	lunedì	*loo-neh-DEE*
money	danaro	*da-NA-ro*
monkey	scimmia	*SHEEM-m'ya*
month	mese (m)	*MEH-zeh*
monument	monumento	*mo-noo-MEN-toh*
moon	luna	*LOO-na*
more	più	*p'yoo*
morning	mattino	*maht-TEE-no*
mosquito	zanzara	*DZAN-dza-ra*
most of . . .	la maggior parte di . . .	*la mahd-JOR PAR-teh dee . . .*
(the) most	il più	*eel p'yoo*
mother	madre (f)	*MA-dreh*
mother-in-law	suocera	*SWO-cheh-ra*
motor	motore (m)	*mo-TOH-reh*
motorcycle	motocicletta	*mo-toh-chee-KLET-ta*
mountain	montagna	*mohn-TAHN-ya*
mouse	topo	*TOH-po*
mouth	bocca	*BOHK-ka*
movie	pellicola	*pel-LEE-ko-la*
movies	cinema	*CHEE-neh-ma*
much	molto	*MOHL-toh*
museum	museo	*moo-ZEH-oh*
music	musica	*MOO-zee-ka*
musician	musicista (m)	*moo-zee-CHEES-ta*

must	dovere	*doh-VEH-reh*

(See use on page 86.)

mustache	baffi (m pl)	*BAHF-fee*
mustard	mostarda	*mo-STAR-da*
my, mine	il mio, la mia, i miei, le mie	*eel MEE-yo, la MEE-ya, ee m'yay, leh MEE-eh*

N

name	nome (m)	*NO-meh*
napkin	tovagliolo	*to-vahl-YO-lo*
narcotics	narcotici	*nar-KO-tee-chee*
narrow	stretto	*STRET-toh*
navy	marina	*ma-REE-na*
near	vicino	*vee-CHEE-no*
necessary	necessario	*neh-chess-SAR-yo*
neck	collo	*KOHL-lo*
necktie	cravatta	*kra-VAHT-ta*
(to) need	aver bisogno (di)	*ah-VAIR bee-ZOHN-yo (dee)*
neighborhood	vicinato	*vee-chee-NA-toh*
nephew	nipote (m)	*nee-PO-teh*
nervous	nervoso	*nair-VO-zo*
neutral	neutrale	*neh-oo-TRA-leh*
never	mai	*my*
Never mind.	Non importa.	*nohn eem-POR-ta.*

new	nuovo	*NWO-vo*
news	notizie (f pl)	*no-TEETS-yeh*
newspaper	giornale (m)	*jor-NA-leh*
next	prossimo	*PROHS-see-mo*
nice	gentile	*jen-TEE-leh*
niece	nipote (f)	*nee-PO-teh*
night	notte (f)	*NOHT-teh*
nightclub	locale notturno	*lo-KA-leh noht-TOOR-no*
nightgown	camicia da notte	*ka-MEE-cha da NOHT-teh*
nine	nove	*NO-veh*
nineteen	diciannove	*dee-chahn-NO-veh*
ninety	novanta	*no-VAHN-ta*
no	no	*no*
nobody	nessuno	*nehs-SOO-no*
noise	rumore (m)	*roo-MO-reh*
none (of them)	nessuno	*nehs-SOO-no*
noon	mezzogiorno	*MED-dzo-JOR-no*
normal	normale	*nor-MA-leh*
north	nord (m)	*nord*
nose	naso	*NA-zo*
not	non	*nohn*
Not yet.	non ancora.	*nohn ahn-KO-ra.*
nothing	niente	*N'YEN-teh*
(to) notice	notare	*no-TA-reh*

noun	nome (m)	*NO-meh*
November	novembre	*no-VEM-breh*
now	adesso	*ah-DESS-so*
nowhere	in nessun posto	*een nes-SOON PO-sto*
number	numero	*NOO-meh-ro*
nurse	infermiera	*een-fairm-YEH-ra*
nuts	noci (m pl)	*NO-chee*

O

occasionally	qualche volta	*KWAHL-keh VOHL-ta*
occupied	occupato	*ohk-koo-PA-toh*
ocean	oceano	*oh-CHEH-ah-no*
o'clock		

(No exact equivalent; see page 32.)

October	ottobre	*oht-TOH-breh*
of	di	*dee*
(to) offer	offrire	*ohf-FREE-reh*
office	ufficio	*oof-FEE-cho*
officer	ufficiale (m)	*oof-fee-CHA-leh*
often	spesso	*SPEHS-so*
oil	olio	*OHL-yo*
O.K.	va bene	*va BEH-neh*
old	vecchio	*VEK-k'yo*

olive	oliva	*oh-LEE-va*
omelet	frittata	*freet-TA-ta*
on	su	*soo*
once	una volta	*OO-na VOHL-ta*
At once!	Subito!	*SOO-bee-toh!*
one	uno	*OO-no*
one way	senso unico	*SEN-so OO-nee-ko*
onion	cipolla	*chee-POHL-la*
only	solo	*SO-lo*
on time	puntuale	*poon-TWA-leh*
onto	sopra	*SO-pra*
open	aperto	*ah-PAIR-toh*
(to) open	aprire	*ah-PREE-reh*
opera	opera	*OH-peh-ra*
opinion	opinione (f)	*oh-peen-YO-neh*
opportunity	opportunità	*ohp-por-too-nee-TA*
opposite	davanti	*da-VAHN-tee*
or	o	*oh*
orange	arancia	*ah-RAHN-cha*
orchestra	orchestra	*or-KESS-tra*
order	ordine (m)	*OR-dee-neh*
in order to	per (followed by the infinitive)	*pair*
(to) order	ordinare	*or-dee-NA-reh*
original	originale	*oh-ree-jee-NAHL-leh*

other	altro	*AHL-tro*
ought to (See "should.")		
our, ours	nostro, la nostra, i nostri, le nostre	*NOHS-tro,* *la NOHS-tra,* *ee NOIIS-troo,* *leh NOHS-treh*
outside	fuori	*FWO-ree*
over	sopra	*SO-pra*
overcoat	cappotto	*kahp-POHT-toh*
over there	laggiù	*luhd-JOO*
overweight (baggage)	peso in più	*PEH-zo een p'yoo*
(to) owe	dovere	*doh-VEH-reh*
own	proprio	*PRO-pr'yo*
owner	proprietario	*pro-pree-yeh-TAR-yo*
ox	bue (m)	*boo WEH*
oyster	ostriche	*OHS-tree-keh*

P

package	pacco	*PAHK-ko*
paid	pagato	*pa-GA-toh*
pain	dolore (m)	*doh-LO-reh*
(to) paint	dipingere	*dee-PEEN-jeh-reh*
painted	dipinto	*dee-PEEN-toh*
painting	quadro	*KWA-dro*
palace	palazzo	*pa-LAHT-tso*

pan	pentola	*PEN-toh-la*
paper	carta	*KAR-ta*
parade	corteo	*kor-TEH-oh*
Pardon me!	Mi scusi!	*mee SKOO-zee!*
park	parco	*PAR-ko*
(to) park	parcheggiare	*par-ked-JA-reh*
parents	genitori	*jeh-nee-TOH-ree*
part	parte (f)	*PAR-teh*
participle	participio	*par-tee-CHEEP-yo*
partner	socio	*SO-cho*
party	festa	*FESS-ta*
passenger	passeggiero	*pahs-sed-JEH-ro*
passport	passaporto	*pahs-sa-POR-toh*
past	passato	*pahs-SA-toh*
(to) pay	pagare	*pa-GA-reh*
peace	pace (f)	*PA-cheh*
pen	penna	*PEN-na*
pencil	matita	*ma-TEE-ta*
people	gente (f)	*JEN-teh*
percent	percento	*pair-CHEN-toh*
perfect	perfetto	*pair-FET-toh*
perfume	profumo	*pro-FOO-mo*
perhaps	forse	*FOR-seh*
permanent	permanente	*pair-ma-NEN-teh*
permitted	permesso	*pair-MESS-so*

person	persona	*pair-SO-na*
photo	fotografia	*fo-toh-gra-FEE-ya*
piano	piano	*P'YA-no*
picture	quadro	*KWA-dro*
piece	pezzo	*PET-tso*
pier	molo	*MO-lo*
pill	pastiglia	*pa-STEEL-ya*
pillow	cuscino	*koo-SHEE-no*
pin	spillo	*SPEEL-lo*
pink	rosa	*RO-za*
pipe	pipa	*PEE-pa*
pistol	pistola	*pees-TOH-la*
place	posto	*PO-sto*
plain (simple)	semplice	*SEM-plee-cheh*
plan	piano	*P'YA-no*
plane	aereo	*ah-EH-reh-yo*
planet	pianeta	*p'ya-NEH-ta*
plant (garden)	pianta	*P'YAHN-ta*
plant (factory)	impianto	*eem-P'YAHN-toh*
plate	piatto	*P'YAHT-toh*
play (theater)	commedia	*kohm-MED-ya*
(to) play	giocare	*jo-KA-reh*
plastic	plastica	*PLAHS-tee-ka*
pleasant	piacevole	*p'ya-CHEH-vo-leh*
please	prego	*PREH-go*

pleasure	piacere (m)	*p'ya-CHEH-reh*
plural	plurale	*ploo-RA-leh*
pocket	tasca	*TA-ska*
poetry	poesia	*po-eh-ZEE-ya*
(to) point	puntare	*poon-TA-reh*
poisonous	velenoso	*veh-leh-NO-zo*
police	polizia	*po-leet-SEE-ya*
policeman	poliziotto	*po-leets-YOHT-toh*
police station	ufficio di polizia	*oo-FEE-cho dee po-leet-SEE-ya*
polite	educato	*eh-doo-KA-toh*
pool	piscina	*pee-SHEE-na*
poor	povero	*PO-veh-ro*
pope	papa (m)	*PA-pa*
popular	popolare	*po-po-LA-reh*
pork	maiale (m)	*ma-YA-leh*
port	porto	*POR-toh*
Portugal	Portogallo	*port-toh-GAHL-lo*
possible	possibile	*pohs-SEE-bee-leh*
postcard	cartolina	*kar-toh-LEE-na*
post office	posta	*PO-sta*
potato	patata	*pa-TA-ta*
pound	libbra	*LEEB-bra*
(to) practice	esercitare	*eh-sair-chee-TA-reh*
(to) prefer	preferire	*preh-feh-REE-reh*

pregnant	incinta	*een-CHEEN-ta*
(to) prepare	preparare	*preh-pa-RA-reh*
present (gift)	regalo	*reh-GA-lo*
president	presidente	*preh-zee-DEN-teh*
(to) press (clothes)	stirare	*stee-RA-reh*
pretty	grazioso	*grahts-YO-zo*
(to) prevent	prevenire	*preh-veh-NEE-reh*
price	prezzo	*PREHT-tso*
priest	prete (m)	*PREH-teh*
prince	principe (m)	*PREEN-chee-peh*
princess	principessa	*preen-chee-PEHS-sa*
principal	principale	*preen-chee-PA-leh*
prison	prigione (f)	*pree-JO-neh*
private	privato	*pree-VA-toh*
probably	probabilmente	*pro-ba-beel-MEN-teh*
problem	problema (m)	*pro-BLEH-ma*
production	produzione (f)	*pro-doots-YO-neh*
profession	professione (f)	*pro-fess-S'YO-neh*
professor	professore (m)	*pro-fess-SO-reh*
profit	profitto	*pro-FEET-toh*
program	programma (m)	*pro-GRAHM-ma*
(to) promise	promettere	*pro-MET-teh-reh*
promised	promesso	*pro-MESS-so*
pronoun	pronome (m)	*pro-NO-meh*

propaganda	propaganda	*pro-pa-GAHN-da*
property	proprietà	*pro-pree-yeh-TA*
Protestant	protestante	*pro-tehs-TAHN-teh*
public	pubblico	*POOB-blee-ko*
publicity	pubblicità	*poob-blee-chee-TA*
publisher	editore (m	*eh-dee-TOH-reh*
(to) pull	tirare	*tee-RA-reh*
pure	puro	*POO-ro*
(to) purchase	comprare	*kohm-PRA-reh*
purple	viola	*V'YO-la*
purse	borsa	*BOR-sa*
(to) push	spingere	*SPEEN-jeh-reh*
(to) put	mettere	*MET-teh-reh*
(to) put on	indossare	*een-dohs-SA-reh*

Q

quality	qualità	*kwa-lee-TA*
queen	regina	*reh-JEE-na*
question	domanda	*doh-MAHN-da*
quick	veloce	*veh-LO-cheh*
quickly	presto	*PRESS-toh*
quiet	quieto	*KW'YEH-toh*
quite	proprio	*PRO-pree-yo*

R

rabbi	rabbino	*rahb-BEE-no*
rabbit	coniglio	*ko-NEEL-yo*
race (contest)	gara	*GA-ra*
radio	radio	*RAHD-yo*
railroad	ferrovia	*fair-ro-VEE-ya*
rain	pioggia	*P'YOHD-ja*
(It's) raining.	Piove.	*P'YO-veh.*
raincoat	impermeabile	*eem-pair-meh-AH-bee-leh*
rapidly	rapidamente	*ra-pee-da-MEN-teh*
rarely	raramente	*ra-ra-MEN-teh*
rate	rata	*RA-ta*
rather	piuttosto	*p'yoot-TOHS-toh*
razor	rasoio	*ra-ZOY-yo*
(to) read	leggere	*LED-jeh-reh*
read (past part.)	letto	*LET-toh*
ready	pronto	*PROHN-toh*
really	veramente	*veh-ra-MEN-teh*
reason	ragione (f)	*ra-JO-neh*
receipt	ricevuta	*ree-cheh-VOO-ta*
(to) receive	ricevere	*ree-CHEH-veh-reh*
recently	recentemente	*reh-chen-teh-MEN-teh*
recipe	ricetta	*ree-CHET-ta*
(to) recognize	riconoscere	*ree-ko-NO-sheh-reh*

(to) recommend	raccomandare	*rahk-ko-mahn-DA-reh*
red	rosso	*ROHS-so*
refrigerator	frigorifero	*free-go-REE-feh-ro*
(to) refuse	rifiutare	*reef-yoo-TA-reh*
(My) regards to ——	Saluti a ——	*sa-LOO-tee ah ——*
regular	regolare	*reh-go-LA-reh*
religion	religione (f)	*reh-lee-JO-neh*
(to) remain	rimanere	*ree-ma-NEH-reh*
(to) remember	ricordare	*ree-kor-DA-reh*
(to) rent	affittare	*ahf-feet-TA-reh*
(to) repair	riparare	*ree-pa-RA-reh*
(to) repeat	ripetere	*ree-PEH-teh-reh*
Repeat, please!	Ripeta, prego!	*ree-PEH-ta, PREH-go!*
report	resoconto	*reh-zo-KOHN-toh*
(to) represent	rappresentare	*rahp-preh-sen-TA-reh*
representative	rappresen-tante (m or f)	*rahp-preh-sen-TAHN-teh*
responsible	responsabile	*reh-spohn-SA-bee-leh*
resident	residente (m)	*reh-see-DEN-teh*
rest (remainder)	resto	*RESS-toh*
(to) rest	riposare	*ree-po-SA-reh*
restaurant	ristorante (m)	*ree-sto-RAHN-teh*
restroom	toeletta	*toh-eh-LET-ta*
(to) return (come back)	ritornare	*ree-tor-NA-reh*

(to) return (give back)	restituire	*reh-stee-too-EE-reh*
revolution	rivoluzione (f)	*ree-vo-loots-YO-neh*
reward	ricompensa	*ree-kohm-PEN-sa*
rice	riso	*REE-zo*
rich	ricco	*REEK-ko*
(to) ride	andare a	*ahn-DA-reh ah*
right (not left)	destro	*DESS-tro*
right (correct)	giusto	*JOO-sto*
Right away!	Subito!	*SOO-bee-toh!*
ring	anello	*ah-NEL-lo*
riot	rivolta	*ree-VOHL-ta*
river	fiume (m)	*F'YOO-meh*
road	strada	*STRA-da*
roof	tetto	*TET-toh*
room	stanza	*STAHNT-sa*
room service	servizio d'al-bergo (m)	*sehr-VEETS-yo dahl-BAIR-go*
round trip	andata e ritorno	*ahn-DA-ta eh ree-TOR-no*
rug	tappeto	*tahp-PEH-toh*
(to) run	correre	*KOR-reh-reh*
Run!	Corra!	*KOR-ra!*
Russia	Russia	*ROOS-s'ya*
Russian	Russo	*ROOS-so*

S

sad	triste	*TREES-teh*
safe (adj)	salvo	*SAHL-vo*
said	detto	*DET-toh*
sailor	marinaio	*ma-ree-NA-yo*
saint	santo (m), santa (f), san (before a masculine name)	*SAHN-toh, SAHN-ta, sahn*
salad	insalata	*èen-sa-LA-ta*
salary	stipendio	*stee-PEND-yo*
sale	vendita	*VEN-dee-ta*
same	stesso	*STEHS-so*
sandwich	panino	*pa-NEE-no*
Saturday	sabato	*SA-ba-toh*
(to) say	dire	*DEE-reh*
scenery	paesaggio	*pye-SAHD-jo*
school	scuola	*SKWO-la*
scissors	forbici	*FOR-bee-chee*
Scotch	scozzese	*skoht-TSEH-zeh*
Scotland	Scozia	*SKOHTS-ya*
sea	mare (m)	*MA-reh*
season	stagione (f)	*sta-JO-neh*
seat	sedile (m)	*seh-DEE-leh*

secretary	segretario (m), -a (f)	seg-reh-TAR-yo, -ya
(to) see	vedere	veh-DEH-reh
(to) seem	sembrare	sem-BRA-reh
It seems ...	Sembra ...	SEM-bra ...
seen	visto	VEES-to
seldom	raramente	ra-ra-MEN-teh
(to) sell	vendere	VEN-deh-reh
(to) send	mandare	mahn-DA-reh
(to) send for	richiedere	ree-K'YEH-deh-reh
September	settembre	set-TEM-breh
serious	serio	SAIR-yo
service	servizio	sair-VEETS-yo
seven	sette	SET-tch
seventeen	diciassette	dee-chahs-SET-teh
seventy	settanta	set-TAHN-ta
several	parecchi	pa-REK-kee
shark	pescecane (m)	peh-sheh-KA-neh
sharp	affilato	ahf-fee-LA-toh
she	essa	ESS-sa
ship	nave (f)	NA-veh
shipment	spedizione (f)	speh-deet-S'YO-neh
shirt	camicia	ka-MEE-cha
shop	negozio	neh-GOHTS-yo
short	corto	KOR-toh

should

I should	dovrei	*dohv-RAY*
you (sg), he, she should	dovrebbe	*dohv-REB-beh*
we should	dovremmo	*dohv-REM-mo*
you (pl), they should	dovrebbero	*dohv-REB-beh-ro*

shoulder	spalla	*SPAHL-la*
show	spettacolo	*spet-TA-ko-lo*
(to) show	mostrare	*mo-STRA-reh*
Show me!	Mi mostri!	*mee MO-stree!*
shower	doccia	*DOHT-cha*
shrimps	scampi (m)	*SKAHM-pee*
shut	chiuso	*K'YOO-zo*
(to) shut	chiudere	*K'YOO-deh-reh*
Sicilian	siciliano	*see-cheel-YA-no*
sick	ammalato	*ahm-ma-LA-toh*
(to) sign	firmare	*feer-MA-reh*
silk	seta	*SEH-ta*
silver	argento	*ar-JEN-toh*
since	da	*da*
sincerely	sinceramente	*seen-cheh-ra-MEN-teh*
(to) sing	cantare	*kahn-TA-reh*
singer	cantante (m, f)	*kahn-TAHN-teh*
sir	signore	*seen-YO-reh*
sister	sorella	*so-REL-la*

sister-in-law	cognata	*kohn-YA-ta*
(Please) sit down.	Si accomodi.	*see ahk-KO-mo-dee*
six	sei	*say*
sixteen	sedici	*SEH-dee-chee*
sixty	sessanta	*sehs-SAHN-ta*
size	misura	*mee-ZOO-ra*
(to) skate	pattinare	*paht-tee-NA-reh*
(to) ski	sciare	*shee-AH-reh*
skirt	gonna	*GOHN-na*
sky	cielo	*CHEH-lo*
(to) sleep	dormire	*dor-MEE-reh*
sleeve	manica	*MA-nee-ka*
slowly	lentamente	*len-ta-MEN-teh*
small	piccolo	*PEEK-ko-lo*
(to) smoke	fumare	*foo-MA-reh*
snow	neve (f)	*NEH-veh*
so	così	*ko-ZEE*
soap	sapone (m)	*sa-PO-neh*
sock	calzetto	*kahld-ZET-toh*
sofa	divano	*dee-VA-no*
soft	soffice	*SOHF-fee-cheh*
soldier	soldato	*sohl-DA-toh*
some (a little)	un po'	*oon po*
some (more than one)	alcuni	*ahl-KOO-nee*
somebody	qualcuno	*kwahl-KOO-no*

something	qualcosa	*kwahl-KO-za*
something else	qualcos'altro	*kwahl-ko-ZAHL-tro*
sometimes	qualche volta	*kwahl-keh VOHL-ta*
somewhere	in qualche posto	*een KWAHL-keh PO-sto*
son	figlio	*FEEL-yo*
son-in-law	genero	*JEN-eh-ro*
song	canzone (f)	*kahnt-SO-neh*
soon	presto	*PRESS-toh*
soprano	soprano	*so-PRA-no*
(I am) sorry.	Mi scusi.	*mee SKOO-zee.*
soup	minestra	*mee-NESS-tra*
south	sud (m)	*sood*
South America	Sud America	*sood ah-MEH-ree-ka*
South American	sudamericano	*sood-ah-meh-ree-KA-no*
souvenir	ricordo	*ree-KOR-doh*
Spain	Spagna	*SPAHN-ya*
Spanish	spagnolo	*spahn-YO-lo*
(to) speak	parlare	*par-LA-reh*
special	speciale	*speh-CHA-leh*
(to) spend	spendere	*SPEN-deh-reh*
spoon	cucchiaio	*kook-K'YA-yo*
sport	sport (m)	*sport*
spring (season)	primavera	*pree-ma-VER-ra*
stairs	scale (f, pl)	*SKA-leh*

stamp	francobollo	*frahn-ko-BOHL-lo*
star	stella	*STEL-la*
(to) start	cominciare	*ko-meen-CHA-reh*
state	stato	*STA-toh*
station	stazione	*stahts-YO-neh*
statue	statua	*STA-too-ah*
(to) stay	stare	*STA-reh*
steak	bistecca	*bees-TEHK-ka*
steel	ferro	*FAIR-ro*
still (adv)	ancora	*ahn-KO-ra*
stocking	calza	*KAHLD-za*
stone	sasso	*SAHS-so*
Stop!	Si fermi!	*see FAIR-mee!*
Stop it!	La smetta!	*la SMET-ta!*
store	negozio	*neh-GOHTS-yo*
storm	temporale (m)	*tem-po-RA-leh*
story	storia	*STOR-ya*
straight	diritto	*dee-REET-toh*
straight ahead	avanti diritto	*ah-VAHN-tee dee-REET-toh*
strange	strano	*STRA-no*
street	strada	*STRA-da*
string	corda	*KOR-da*
strong	forte	*FOR-teh*
student	studente (m or f)	*stoo-DEN-teh*

(to) study	studiare	*stoo-D'YA-reh*
style	stile (m)	*STEE-leh*
subway	metropolitana	*meh-tro-po-lee-TA-na*
suddenly	improvvisa-mente	*eem-prohv-vee-za-MEN-teh*
sugar	zucchero	*DZOOK-keh-ro*
suit	vestito	*ves-TEE-toh*
suitcase	valigia	*va-LEE-ja*
summer	estate (f)	*es-TA-teh*
sun	sole (m)	*SO-leh*
Sunday	domenica	*do-MEH-nee-ka*
sure	sicuro	*see-KOO-ro*
surely	sicuramente	*see-koo-ra-MEN-teh*
surprise	sorpresa	*sor-PREH-za*
sweater	maglione	*mahl-YO-neh*
sweet	dolce	*DOHL-cheh·*
(to) swim	nuotare	*nwo-TA-reh*
swimming pool	piscina	*pee-SHEE-na*
Swiss	svizzero	*ZVEET-tseh-ro*
Switzerland	Svizzera	*ZVEET-tseh-ra*

T

table	tavola	*TA-vo-la*
tablecloth	tovaglia	*toh-VAHL-ya*
tailor	sarto	*SAR-toh*

(to) take	prendere	*PREN-deh-reh*
(to) take away	ritirare	*ree-tee-RA-reh*
(to) take a walk, take a ride	passeggiare	*pahs-sed-JA-reh*
(to) talk	parlare	*par-LA-reh*
tall	alto	*AHL-toh*
tank	serbatoio	*ser-ba-TOY-yo*
tape	nastro	*NA-stro*
tape recorder	registratore	*reh-jee-stra-TOH-reh*
tax	tassa	*TAHS-sa*
taxi	tassì (m)	*tahs-SEE*
tea	tè (m)	*teh*
(to) teach	insegnare	*een-sehn-YA-reh*
teacher	insegnante (m or f)	*een-sen-YAHN-teh*
team	squadra	*SKWA-dru*
telegram	telegramma (m)	*teh-leh-GRAHM-ma*
telephone	telefono	*teh-LEH-fo-no*
television	televisione (f)	*teh-leh-vees-YO-neh*
(to) tell	dire	*DEE-reh*
Tell him (her) that . . .	Gli (le) dica che . . .	*l'yee (leh) DEE-ka keh . . .*
temperature	temperatura	*tem-peh-ra-TOO-ra*
ten	dieci	*D'YEH-chee*
tenor	tenore (m)	*teh-NO-reh*
terrace	terrazza	*tair-RAHT-tza*

terrible	terribile	*tair-REE-bee-leh*
than	che	*keh*
thank you	grazie	*GRAHTS-yeh*
that (pron)	quello	*KWEL-lo*
that (conj)	che	*keh*
the	il, la	*eel, la* (See the introduction to dictionary.)
theater	teatro	*teh-AH-tro*
their, theirs	il loro, la loro, i loro, le loro	*eel (la, ee, leh) LO-ro*
them	li (m), le (f), loro	*lee, leh, LO-ro*
then	allora	*ahl-LO-ra*
there	là	*la*
there is . . .	c'è . . .	*cheh . . .*
there are . . .	ci sono . . .	*chee SO-no . . .*
these (adj)	questi	*KWESS-tee*
they	essi (m), esse (f)	*ESS-see, ESS-seh*
thin	magro	*MA-gro*
thing	cosa	*KO-za*
(to) think	pensare	*pen-SA-reh*
Do you think that . . . ?	Pensa che . . . ?	*PEN-sa keh . . . ?*
third	terzo	*TAIRT-so*
thirteen	tredici	*TREH-dee-chee*
thirty	trenta	*TRAIN-ta*

this	questo	*KWESS-toh*
those	quelli	*KWEL-lee*
thousand	mille	*MEEL-leh*
thread	filo	*FEE-lo*
three	tre	*treh*
throat	gola	*GO-la*
through	attraverso	*aht-tra-VAIR-so*
Thursday	giovedì	*jo-veh-DEE*
ticket	biglietto	*beel-YET-toh*
tie	cravatta	*kra-VAHT-ta*
tiger	tigre (m)	*TEE-greh*
time	ora	*OH-ra*
tip	mancia	*MAHN-cha*
tire	pneumatico	*p'neh-oo-MA-tee-ko*
tired	stanco	*STAHN-ko*
to (direction)	a	*ah*
to (in order to)	per	*pair*
toast	pane tostato	*PA-neh toh-STA-toh*
tobacco	tabacco	*ta-BAHK-ko*
today	oggi	*OHD-jee*
toe	dito del piede	*DEE-toh del P'YEH-deh*
together	insieme	*eens-YEH-meh*
tomato	pomodoro	*po-mo-DOH-ro*
tomb	tomba	*TOHM-ba*
tongue	lingua	*LEEN-gwa*

tonight	stanotte	*sta-NOHT-teh*
too (also)	anche	*AHN-keh*
too (excessive)	troppo	*TRÓHP-po*
tool	strumento	*stroo-MEN-toh*
tooth	dente (m)	*DEN-teh*
toothbrush	spazzolino da denti	*spaht-tso-LEE-no da DEN-tee*
toothpaste	dentifricio	*den-tee-FREE-cho*
tour	giro	*JEE-ro*
tourist	turista	*too-REES-ta*
toward	verso	*VAIR-so*
towel	asciugamano	*ah-shoo-ga-MA-no*
tower	torre (f)	*TOHR-reh*
town	città	*cheet-TA*
toy	giocattolo	*jo-KAHT-toh-lo*
traffic	traffico	*TRAHF-fee-ko*
train	treno	*TREH-no*
translation	traduzione	*tra-doots-YO-neh*
(to) travel	viaggiare	*v'yahd-JA-reh*
travel agent	agente di viaggio	*ah-JEN-teh dee V'YAHD-jo*
traveler	viaggiatore	*v'yahd-ja-TOH-reh*
treasurer	tesoriere	*teh-zor-YEH-reh*
tree	albero	*AHL-beh-ro*
trip	viaggio	*V'YAHD-jo*
trouble	disturbo	*dee-STOOR-bo*

trousers	pantaloni (m pl)	*pahn-ta-LO-nee*
truck	camion (m)	*KAHM-yohn*
true	vero	*VEH-ro*
truth	verità	*veh-ree-TA*
(to) try	provare	*pro-VA-reh*
(to) try on	indossare	*een-dohs-SA-reh*
Tuesday	martedì	*mar-teh-DEE*
Turkey	Turchia	*toor-KEE-ya*
Turkish	turco	*TOOR-ko*
(to) turn	girare	*Jee-RA-reh*
(to) turn off	spegnere	*SPEN-yeh-reh*
(to) turn on	accendere	*aht-CHEN-deh-reh*
twelve	dodici	*DOH-dee-chee*
two	due	*DOO-weh*
typewriter	macchina da scrivere	*MAHK-kee-na da SKREE-veh-reh*
typical	tipico	*TEE-pee-ko*

U

ugly	brutto	*BROOT-toh*
umbrella	ombrello	*ohm-BREL-lo*
uncle	zio	*DZEE-oh*
under	sotto	*SOHT-toh*
(to) understand	capire	*ka-PEE-reh*

Do you understand?	Capisce?	ka-PEE-sheh?
I don't understand.	Non capisco.	nohn ka-PEES-ko.
understood	capito	ka-PEE-toh
underwear	biancheria personale	b'yahn-keh-REE-ah pair-so-NA-leh
unfortunately	sfortunata- mente	sfor-too-na-ta-MEN- teh
uniform	uniforme (m)	oo-nee-FOR-meh
United States	Stati Uniti	STA-tee oo-NEE-tee
United Nations	Nazioni Unite	nahdz-YO-nee oo- NEE-teh
university	università	oo-nee-ver-see-TA
until	fino	FEE-no
up	su	soo
urgent	urgente	oor-JEN-teh
us (object)	ci	chee
us (with prep)	noi	noy
(to) use	usare	oo-ZA-reh
used to (in the habit of)	abituato a	ah-beet-WA-toh ah
useful	utile	OO-tee-leh
usually	di solito	dee SO-lee-toh

V

| vacant | libero | LEE-beh-ro |
| vacation | vacanza | va-KAHN-dza |

vaccination	vaccino	*vaht-CHEE-no*
valley	valle (f)	*VAHL-leh*
valuable	di valore	*dee va-LO-reh*
value	valore	*va-LO-reh*
vanilla	vaniglia	*va-NEEL-ya*
various	vario	*VAR-yo*
veal	vitello	*vee-TEL-lo*
vegetable	verdura	*vair-DOO-ra*
verb	verbo	*VAIR-bo*
very	molto	*MOHL-toh*
very well	molto bene	*MOHL-toh BEH-neh*
view	vista	*VEES-ta*
village	villaggio	*veel-LAHD-jo*
vinegar	aceto	*ah-CHEH-toh*
visa	visto	*VEES-toh*
visit	visita	*vee-ZEE-ta*
(to) visit	visitare	*vee-zee-TA-reh*
violin	violino	*vee-yo-LEE-no*
vivid	vivido	*VEE-vee-doh*
voice	voce (f)	*VO-cheh*
volcano	vulcano	*vool-KA-no*
voyage	viaggio	*V'YAHD-jo*

W

waist	vita	*VEE-ta*

(to) wait	aspettare	*ah-spet-TA-reh*
Wait here!	Aspetti qui!	*ah-SPET-tee kweel*
waiter	cameriere	*ka-mair-YEH-reh*
waitress	cameriera	*ka-mair-YEH-ra*
(to) walk	camminare	*kahm-mee-NA-reh*
wall	muro	*MOO-ro*
wallet	portafoglio	*por-ta-FOHL-yo*
(to) want	volere	*vo-LEH-reh*
I want	voglio	*VOHL-yo*
you (sg) want	Lei vuole	*lay VWO-leh*
he, she wants	vuole	*VWO-leh*
we want	vogliamo	*vohl-YA-mo*
you (pl) want	Loro vogliono	*LO-ro VOHL-yo-no*
they want	vogliono	*VOHL-yo-no*
Do you want . . . ?	Vuole . . . ?	*VWO-leh . . . ?*
Does he (she) want . . . ?	Vuole . . . ?	*VWO-leh . . . ?*
war	guerra	*GWAIR-ra*
warm	caldo	*KAHL-doh*
was		
I was	ero	*EH-ro*
he, she was	era	*EH-ra*
(to) wash	lavare	*la-VA-reh*
watch	orologio	*oh-ro-LO-jo*
Watch out!	Attento!	*aht-TEN-toh!*

water	acqua	*AHK-kwa*
water color	acquerello	*ahk-kweh-REL-lo*
way (manner)	modo	*MO-doh*
way (road))	strada	*STRA-da*
we	noi	*noy*
weak	debole	*DEH-bo-leh*
(to) wear	indossare	*een-dohs-SA-reh*
weather	tempo	*TEM-po*
wedding	matrimonio	*ma-tree-MOHN-yo*
week	settimana	*set-tee-MA-na*
weekend	fine settimana	*FEE-neh set-tee-MA-na*
(to) weigh	pesare	*peh-SA-reh*
weight	peso	*PEH-zo*
Welcome!	Benvenuto!	*ben-ven-NOO-toh!*
You are welcome.	Prego.	*PREH-go.*
well	bene	*BEH-neh*
went		
I went	sono andato, -ta	*SO-no ahn-DA-toh, -ta*
you (sg) went	Lei è andato, -ta	*lay eh ahn-DA-toh, -ta*
he, she went	è andato, -ta	*eh ahn-DA-toh, -ta*
we went	siamo andati, -te	*S'YA-mo ahn-DA-tee, -teh*
you (pl) went	Loro sono andati, -te	*LO-ro SO-no ahn-DA-tee, -teh*

they went	sono andati, -te	SO-no ahn-DA-tee, -teh
were		
you (sg) were	Lei era	lay EH-ra
we were	eravamo	eh-ra-VA-mo
you (pl) were	Loro erano	LO-ro EH-ra-no
they were	erano	EH-ra-no
west	ovest	OH-vest
what?	cosa?	KO-za?
What's the matter?	Cosa è successo?	KO-za eh soot-CHEHS-so?
What time is it?	Che ora è?	keh OH-ra eh?
What do you want?	Cosa desidera?	KO-za deh-ZEE-deh-ra?
wheel	ruota	R'WO-ta
when	quando	KWAHN-doh
where	dove	DOH-veh
Where is . . . ?	Dov'è . . . ?	doh-VEH . . . ?
which	quale	KWA-leh
while	mentre	MEN-treh
white	bianco	B'YAHN-ko
who	chi	kee
whole	intero	een-TEH-ro
whom	chi	kee
why?	perchè?	pair-KEH

Why not?	Perchè no?	*pair-KEH no?*
wide	largo	*LAR-go*
widow	vedova	*VEH-doh-va*
widower	vedovo	*VEH-doh-vo*
wife	moglie (f)	*MOHL-yeh*
wild	selvaggio	*sel-VAHD-jo*

will: The future is formed by adding one of the following endings, according to the subject, to the stem of the verb. For a verb whose infinitive ends in -are or -ere: (io) -erò, (Lei, egli, ella) -erà, (noi) -eremo, (Loro, essi, esse) -eranno. For a verb whose infinitive ends in -ire: (io) -irò, (Lei, egli, ella) -irà, (noi) -iremo, (Loro, essi, esse) -iranno.

I will speak	parlerò	*par-leh-RO*
he will understand	capirà	*ka-pee-RA*
he won't understand	non capirà	*nohn ka-pee-RA*

(to) win	vincere	*VEEN-cheh-reh*
wind	vento	*VEN-toh*
window	finestra	*fee-NEHS-tra*
wine	vino	*VEE-no*
winter	inverno	*cen-VAIR-no*
(to) wish	desiderare	*deh-zee-deh-RA-reh*
without	senza	*SENT-sa*
wolf	lupo	*LOO-po*
woman	donna	*DOHN-na*
wonderful	meraviglioso	*meh-ra-veel-YO-zo*

won't (See "will.")

wood	legno	*LEN-yo*
woods	bosco	*BOHS-ko*
wool	lana	*LA-na*
word	parola	*pa-RO-la*
work	lavoro	*la-VO-ro*
(to) work	lavorare	*la-vo-RA-reh*
world	mondo	*MOHN-doh*
Don't worry!	Non si pre- occupi!	*nohn see preh-OHK- koo-pee!*
worse	peggio	*PED-jo*

would: Express the idea of "would" by adding the appropriate one of the following endings to the stem of the verb. For a verb whose infinitive ends in -are or ere: (io) -erei, (Lei, egli, ella) -erebbe, (noi) -eremmo, (Loro, essi, esse) -erebbero. For a verb whose infinitive ends in -ire: (io) -irei, (Lei, egli, ella) -irebbe, (noi) -iremmo, (Loro, essi, esse) -irebbero.

I would try	proverei	*pro-veh-RAY*
he would open	aprirebbe	*ah-pree-REB-beh*
I would like	vorrei	*vohr-RAY*
Would you, he, she like . . . ?	Le piacereb- be . . . ?	*leh p'ya-cheh-REB- beh . . . ?*

wrist	polso	*POHL-so*
(to) write	scrivere	*SKREE-veh-reh*
writer	scrittore (m)	*skreet-TOR-reh*
Write it!	Lo scriva!	*lo SKREE-va!*

| wrong | sbagliato | *zbahl-YA-toh* |

Y

year	anno	*AHN-no*
yellow	giallo	*JAHL-lo*
yes	sì	*see*
yesterday	ieri	*YEH-ree*
yet	ancora	*ahn-KO-ra*

you (See introduction to the dictionary.)

(as subject)	Lei, tu (sg); Loro, voi (pl)	*lay, too, LO-ro, voy*
(as object)	La, ti (sg); Li, vi	*la, tee, lee, vee*
young	giovane	*JO-va-neh*
your, yours (sg)	il Suo, la Sua, i Suoi, le Sue	*eel SOO-wo, la SOO-wa, ee swoy, leh SOO-eh*
your, yours (pl)	il Loro, la Loro, i Loro, le Loro	*eel (la, ee, leh) LO-ro*
Yugoslavia	Jugoslavia	*yoo-go-SLAHV-ya*

Z

zipper	chiusura lampo	*k'yoo-ZOO-ra LAHM-po*
zone	zona	*DZO-na*
zoo	zoo	*dzo-oh*

Point to the Answer

For speedy reference and, when in doubt, to get a clear answer to a question you have just asked, show the following sentences to the person you are addressing and let *him* point to the answer.

Notare questo per favore: Per avere la sicurezza di 'essere capito, vi prego di mostrare la risposta alla domanda sulla pagina presentata.

Sì. Yes.	**No.** No.	**Forse.** Perhaps.
Certamente. Certainly.	**Va bene.** All right.	**Mi scusi.** Excuse me.
Capisco. I understand.	**Non capisco.** I don't understand.	
Cosa desidera? What do you want?	**Lo so.** I know.	**Non lo so.** I don't know.
Ancora. Again (or) More.	**Basta così.** Enough.	

Aperto.   **Chiuso.**   **Troppo.**   **Non è sufficiente.**
Open.   Closed.   Too much.   Not enough.

Vietato entrare.   **Proibito.**
No admittance.   It is forbidden.

Proprietà privata.   **Lei deve andarsene.**
Private property.   You must leave.

Adesso.   **Più tardi.**   **Troppo presto.**
Now.   Later.   Too early.

Troppo tardi.	Oggi.	Domani.	Ieri.
Too late.	Today.	Tomorrow.	Yesterday.

Questa sera.	Ieri sera.	Domani sera.
Tonight.	Last night.	Tomorrow night.

Questa settimana.	La settimana scorsa.
This week.	Last week.

La prossima settimana.	È possibile.	Non è possibile.
Next week.	It's possible.	It's not possible.

D'accordo.	Benissimo.	Non va bene.
It is agreed.	Very good.	It isn't good.

È vicino.	Troppo lontano.	Molto lontano.
It's near.	Too far.	Very far.

Qui.	Là.
Here.	There.

Giri a sinistra.	Giri a destra.
Turn left.	Turn right.

Vada diritto.	Venga con me.
Go straight ahead.	Come with me.

Mi segua.	Andiamo.
Follow me.	Let's go.

Siamo arrivati.	Si fermi qui.	Mi aspetti.
We have arrived.	Stop here.	Wait for me.

Non posso.	Aspetto.	Devo andare.
I cannot.	I will wait.	I must go.

Torni più tardi.	Torno subito.
Come back later.	I'll be right back.

Io mi chiamo ———.
My name is ———.

E lei?
And you?

Il numero di telefono.
Telephone number.

Indirizzo.
Address.

lunedì	martedì	mercoledì	giovedì
Monday	Tuesday	Wednesday	Thursday

venerdì	sabato	domenica
Friday	Saturday	Sunday

Alle ———.
At ——— o'clock.

Costa ——— lire.
It costs ——— lire.

uno	due	tre	quattro	cinque
one	two	three	four	five

sei	sette	otto	nove	dieci
six	seven	eight	nine	ten

undici	dodici	tredici	quattordici
eleven	twelve	thirteen	fourteen

quindici	sedici	diciassette	diciotto
fifteen	sixteen	seventeen	eighteen

diciannove	venti	trenta	quaranta
nineteen	twenty	thirty	forty

cinquanta	sessanta	settanta	ottanta
fifty	sixty	seventy	eighty

novanta	cento
ninety	one hundred

mille	diecimila
one thousand	ten thousand